D1312923

BRENT LIBRARIES

9112000041 5402

STEPHEN HAWKING

Nikki Sheehan

Illustrated by Mike Phillips

SCHOLASTIC

For Frank Sheehan.

First published in the UK by Scholastic Children's Books, 2019
Euston House, 24 Eversholt Street, London, NW1 1DB
A division of Scholastic Limited

London – New York – Toronto – Sydney - Auckland
Mexico City – New Delhi – Hong Kong

SCHOLASTIC and associated logos are trademarks and/or registered
trademarks of Scholastic Inc.

Text © Nikki Sheehan, 2019
Cover illustration by Sarah Papworth
Text illustrations by Mike Phillips

The right of Nikki Sheehan to be identified as the author of this
work respectively has been asserted by them in accordance with the
Copyright, Designs and Patents Act, 1988.

ISBN 978 1407 19318 2

Any we'   ing
to print.   inge
and webs   . We

CONTENTS

INTRODUCTION

. . . .

This is a book about a man who travelled within his own mind back to the creation of the universe. And then he set out to help ordinary people, like you and me, to understand space, time and beyond. He wanted you to look up at the stars and marvel at our universe, so, although you may be expecting to read about the life of scientist Stephen Hawking, we are going to start with how he and you, and the book you are reading, all began. Because, somewhere within the life of this one great man, lies the story of everything.

USEFUL WORDS

There are lots of tricky words used in the world of science. Here are some useful definitions to help you understand the concepts in this book. There are more useful words in the glossary at the back of the book!

A particle: a tiny piece of matter

Atom: the basic building block for all matter in the universe

Big Bang theory: the theory that states that the universe expanded out of a singularity

Black hole: a region in space with gravity so strong that everything, even light, is sucked inside

Dark matter: an invisible matter (stuff!) found in 90 per cent of the universe

Galaxy: a group of stars, gas and dust and their solar system

Gravity: a force that tries to pull objects towards each other

Light year: a unit of measurement used in astronomy, to measure the distance light travels in a year (which is equal to 5.88 trillion miles / 9.5 trillion kilometres)

Mass: the amount of matter in an object

Matter: anything that has mass and takes up space is made up of matter

Singularity: an object with so much gravity it squeezes everything inside it down to a single point

Star: a ball of gas held together by its own gravity

Universe: all of the galaxies and everything in between

IN THE BEGINNING...

Imagine nothing at all. Absolutely nothing.

Not just no dogs or cats or people, or houses or roads or schools. Nothing.

Imagine no Earth to stand on, no Sun to warm you, no sky above you, no air around you, no gravity to hold you, no light to help you see, no darkness to keep you blind.

Imagine a time when there wasn't even any space where something could exist. Let's date this time before time began, although in reality time didn't exist yet. Let's call it 13.8 billion years ago.

And then, let's suppose that from nothing and for no apparent reason, time, the universe and everything exploded into existence.

This nothing-to-something process was fast.

BANG!

At first the universe, time and everything was very small. If you'd been there – which of course you couldn't have as you didn't exist – you wouldn't have noticed a change. Because everything began as a dot smaller than a pinhead, called a "singularity". But – and this is where it gets harder to believe – that tiny dot contained as much "everything" as exists in the whole universe today. Squeezed into the tiny and very overcrowded dot was all the matter and energy that makes you and me and the ground we stand on, the skies and the planets, even all of the gravity, electricity and even magnetism.

Absolutely everything.

It was like a sponge, squeezed tightly in your hand. The space the sponge takes up may be smaller than usual, but its mass (the amount of sponge) is the same. And all the time the sponge (and the universe!) is waiting to expand.

And so this pinhead universe couldn't exist for long, and after a hundredth of a billionth of a trillionth of a trillionth of a second the universe expanded again. Not much, just to the size of a ping-pong ball. But then, a few seconds later, the *really* amazing thing happened: it grew into the size of a whole galaxy! And then, on and on the universe continued to expand, and is still expanding today.

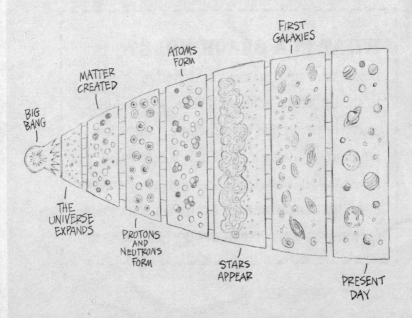

FIRST GALAXIES

ATOMS FORM

MATTER CREATED

BIG BANG

THE UNIVERSE EXPANDS

PROTONS AND NEUTRONS FORM

STARS APPEAR

PRESENT DAY

This is what's known as the Big Bang theory. It's only a theory because it's hard to prove, but most scientists now agree that it's the most likely beginning to the universe.

But at that time, 13.8 billion years and just a few seconds ago, it wasn't a universe that we would recognize. It was a hot black mess of particles, like a vast terrifying soup. But changes were happening. All sorts of matter was busy forming: tiny particles, protons, neutrons, photons and neutrinos, all swimming around the giant cosmic bowl of universe soup.

WHAT IS A BLACK HOLE?

Black holes are the most destructive objects in the universe. Scientists believe that – like at the beginning of the universe – there is a singularity inside a black hole where gravity is so strong that anything that gets near enough, even light, is never seen again. We don't know for sure what it's like in a black hole because anyone who fell inside would be stretched through a process called "spaghettification". This is probably less fun than it sounds. So far our knowledge of black holes has been largely theoretical, but recently the world was astonished to see the first real image of one: a silhouette of a black hole 55 million light years from Earth, named M87, which was captured by a team of 200 scientists using eight telescopes around the world.

SPAGHETTIFICATION

Also known as the "noodle effect", this is not as delicious as it sounds! It's what happens to an object when super-strength gravity stretches and squeezes it into a long, thin string shape.

So, in just sixteen minutes, all the particles of matter that exist today had formed. But this "soup" was still too hot and after the speedy beginning things slowed down considerably. There was a 380,000-year wait while the universe cooled down and the building blocks of everything in the universe, called atoms, were able to form. But it was worth waiting for because amazing things happened.

First, light, which had been trapped by the loose electrons,

Then the universe that we can now see from Earth expanded until it was millions of light years across. The fog cleared and the beautiful universe was transparent.

It was no longer a black soup. But, if you had been there, all you would have seen was a fading red glow, becoming dimmer as the universe continued to grow and stretch the wavelengths of the photons. And then, just when things were going so well, as if someone had flicked a switch, the light went out, and there was only darkness.

It may have looked like the universe had emptied but, fortunately, it hadn't. The universe was actually filled with matter, but it was mostly dark matter that couldn't produce light and therefore couldn't be seen. The universe had entered what's known as the Cosmic Dark Ages.

As if exhausted from all the action, the universe seemed to rest for a while. Quite a while – a few hundred million years! But small changes were still happening. Microscopic ripples in the dark matter meant that it had become unevenly spread, and some areas had more mass. Slowly, gravity pulled these denser patches of dark matter and gas together, allowing them to collide and merge with other dense patches. Collapsing gas clouds began to break down into dense blobs that were so hot that they started to release nuclear energy.

And then, eventually, the darkness was broken as one of these blobs burst into light and the first star was born. The universe as we know it was beginning.

BUT HOW DO WE KNOW?

Today there is still a faint glow in space from the Big Bang. Scientists on board spacecraft can see this as a pattern of slightly warmer and cooler gas all around us, with ripples showing where the hydrogen clouds were slightly denser.

A STAR IS BORN

Bring your minds all the way forward now to 1942. The nothingness, Big Bang and Cosmic Dark Ages are way behind us. By 1942, the first stars had died and Earth has been formed for 4.54 billion years. (We'll come back to how that happened in "Daring to Dream".)

The important thing is that by 1942, life on Earth had begun. Humans had been around for 200,000 years, and soon discovered fire, tools, farming and governments, and then began working towards creating airplanes, tanks and guns so they could fight each other more efficiently.

So, in 1942, the world is three years into the biggest war in its history, World War II, and intelligent, resourceful, modern humanity is busy trying to destroy itself.

It was not a good time to be born in London. German troops were in France, just across the

English Channel, as well as in Poland, Holland, Belgium, Denmark, Norway and Luxembourg. Although no fighting was happening in England, people were on edge after the nightly bombing of the main British towns and cities – the Blitz.

The terror of the Blitz had finished in May 1941, but London was in ruins. More than a million homes had been destroyed or damaged by bombs, and danger still remained for ordinary Londoners.

THE BLITZ

Blitz means "lightning" in German. It's the name given to a nightly attack on British cities that lasted from September 1940 to May 1941. Only one night was missed in over 11 weeks and 44,652 civilians were killed and 52,370 were seriously injured.

Mr and Mrs Hawking

One young couple, Isobel and Frank Hawking, were especially worried at this time because they were expecting their first child.

Isobel Hawking, Stephen's mother, was very unusual for the time because her parents had allowed her to go to Oxford University in the 1930s. Back then, women were not encouraged to study and once they were married they were expected to be satisfied with being a wife and mother instead of having a career and earning their own money.

WOMEN AT UNIVERSITY

Although women had attended lectures at Oxford University since the 1870s, they weren't allowed to graduate (be given a degree) – even if they had passed all the exams – until 1920.

Isobel was a very intelligent, hard-working woman, and she graduated with a degree in Philosophy, Politics and Economics (PPE), which is thought of as incredibly difficult.

But, because she was a woman, a degree from Oxford didn't help Isobel to have a high-level career. Eventually, she took a job as a medical secretary at the National Institute for Medical Research. Fortunately for the world, it was there that Isobel met the man who would become Stephen's father – Frank Hawking.

NOT ALL ASTRONOMERS ARE MEN!

Although history has tended to focus on male scientists, many women made important discoveries, too. The person who found out what the universe was made of was a British-born woman called Cecilia Payne-Gaposchkin. She discovered that the most plentiful atom in the universe is hydrogen.

Cecilia also discovered what the Sun is made of, but sadly a man named Henry Norris

Russell is usually given the credit for this. In fact, he knew about her findings and told her not to publish them, then four years later published the very same results!

Like Stephen, Cecilia attended Cambridge University – she won a scholarship to Newnham College in 1919. But back in the 1920s Cambridge wouldn't award women their degrees. So, Cecilia moved to America in 1923 and eventually became a professor at the famous Harvard University. It's thanks to Cecilia that scientists know anything about variable stars (the ones that twinkle). Almost all studies on these stars are based on her work. Cecilia has inspired generations of women to work in the sciences and she should not be forgotten.

Frank was older than Isobel and had also graduated from Oxford. He was an epidemiologist (someone who studies diseases) and had been working in Africa when World War II began. At that time all men were expected to join the army to defend their country, so Frank did so. But instead of sending him to fight, the army gave him a medical research job.

Frank and Isobel married quickly after they met, and soon they learned that they were going to become parents. Fortunately for the Hawkings, they knew a place, away from the dangers of war, for Isobel to give birth. The Germans had agreed not to target the university towns of Oxford and Cambridge if Britain didn't bomb Heidelberg and Göttingen, the German university towns.

So, the Hawkings went to stay in a hotel in Oxford to wait for a very special arrival. And, on 8 January 1942, on the 300th anniversary of the death of the famous scientist Galileo Galilei, they welcomed into the world one of the greatest scientists the world has ever known: Stephen William Hawking.

GALILEO GALILEI

Stephen Hawking liked to think that being born on Galileo's 300th "deathversary" had influenced him to become an astronomer.

Galileo was one of Stephen's lifelong favourite scientists. Young Stephen liked to read about how Galileo used a telescope to prove that the planets revolved around the Sun rather than the Earth, as was taught by the powerful Catholic Church at that time – and how Galileo was forced by the Church to deny what he had found. Later on in his life, Stephen was able to put this injustice right.

All Children Are Different

Stephen Hawking was not always a great scientist. He began, according to his mother, as a very normal child.

His earliest memory came from when he was only two and a half. The family had moved back to London after Stephen was born and were living in a north London suburb, Highgate. According to Stephen, he was standing in front of his nursery at his first school, Byron House, and crying his head off! It was the first time that Stephen had been left with people he didn't know and, although he wanted to join in with all the children playing around him, he was too afraid. His parents were surprised because being bookish people, they had read child development textbooks and had learnt that this was the right age for their son to start making friends. Stephen showed them, however, that all children are different. They took their son away and didn't make him go back to school until he was four years old.

Stephen's home at that time was a tall, narrow Victorian house, which his parents had bought very cheaply when everyone thought that the area was going to be bombed flat. Before he was even two years old, Stephen's sister Mary was born. Meanwhile, the war was still raging and once, when Stephen was away from home with his mother and baby sister, a German V-2 rocket landed a few houses away, leaving a huge crater in the street. Fortunately, the Hawkings' house wasn't badly damaged and Frank, who was home at the time, wasn't injured. Maybe because of this, the family felt lucky to have a home that was still standing and they often invited people whose houses had been destroyed to stay with them..

THE V-2 ROCKET – AND SPACE!

V-2 rockets were particularly dangerous because they arrived silently and flew too fast to be shot down by the anti-aircraft guns of fighter aircraft. V-2s killed several thousand people, but in the end didn't help Hitler to win the war. However, the rocket did help the Americans to get their first man into space. The German engineer who designed the V-2, Wernher von Braun, was taken to America after the war where he developed the V-2 into a rocket that in 1961 took Alan Shepard, America's first astronaut, into space.

Stargazer

Young Stephen's house was always full of adults, many of them very clever and scientific people having interesting conversations. Although he may have been too young to join in, Stephen's parents raised him to always be curious – to ask questions and try to work out the answers.

One subject that young Stephen had many questions about was space. Before he was old enough for physics lessons at school, Stephen would lie under the night sky and gaze upwards. He was desperate to know more about the far depths of the universe.

SCINTILLATING SCIENCES

The science subjects you are likely to study in school are:

Biology: the study of all living things

Chemistry: the study of what matter is made of and how it reacts with other substances

Physics: the part of science that studies matter and energy and how they work together.

Astronomers and cosmologists such as Stephen use knowledge gained from physics, chemistry and even biology (if they are searching for alien life!) in their work.

Stephen's scientific mind extended to his choice of toys. Because of the war there were few opportunities for his family to buy three-year-old Stephen the playthings he wanted. The factories needed all raw materials – like metal and rubber – to make things such as weapons and gas masks. The few toys that were produced were made out of leftovers from factories, but metal was mostly saved for military use.

Model trains were mostly metallic, so they were especially hard to find. This was a problem for Stephen who was crazy about trains and how they worked. His father tried to make him a basic one from wood, but Stephen wanted a train that moved on its own. So, his father somehow found a broken secondhand clockwork train, which he repaired with a soldering iron and gave to Stephen for Christmas 1945, when he was nearly four. It didn't work very well, but it kept Stephen happy.

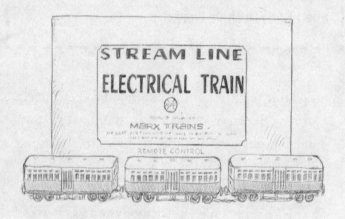

It wasn't until the war was over that Stephen's father went on a trip to America and brought back a model train, complete with a figure-of-eight track. Even as an old man Stephen still remembered how excited he was when he opened the box.

SCRAP METAL

Many of the metal railings outside of people's houses were melted down for use in the war effort. Today, you can still see the stumps where they were cut off. Sadly, it's believed that the government was unable to melt down the huge quantity collected and a lot of the metal that was removed in London was dumped into the River Thames, where it remains today.

Following the war, metal railings outside of London's housing estates were often replaced with old, metal stretchers used to carry injured people during the Blitz.

Model Builder

As he grew older, Stephen's fascination with trains didn't fade but rather became more sophisticated. He spent hours watching a model railway club in

Crouch End, London. He had moved on from clockwork trains that had to be wound up with a key, and dreamt of getting an electric train set.

Finally, Stephen found his chance. He had a small amount of money saved up and when his parents were away, he spent it all on the electric train set of his dreams.

Unfortunately, when he got it home he realized that it didn't work very well. Stephen began to understand that if he wanted working models that he could really control, he was going to have to start building them himself.

As a teenager Stephen began to do this, starting with aeroplanes and boats. He wasn't very skilled with his hands, but he had a good school friend, John McClenahan, who was much better at modelling than him. John also had a workshop that they could use. Stephen didn't really care what his models looked like – it was the fun of creating them that drove him to keep on trying.

Stephen's love of tinkering wasn't restricted to vehicles. When his sister, Mary, was given a doll's house as a present Stephen got to work improving it by adding plumbing and electricity.

By now Stephen wasn't only making models. With another school friend, Roger Ferneyhough, Stephen invented a range of board games, based on manufacturing and war, and even one about a group of landowners and peasant workers. He said that he made these games, as well as the trains, boats and aeroplanes, because he had a need to know how systems worked and how to control them. He later used this curiosity in his research into the universe. He was known to have thought,

"IF YOU UNDERSTAND HOW THE UNIVERSE WORKS, YOU CONTROL IT, IN A WAY."

NO TV?

Very few homes had televisions or even telephones when Stephen was growing up, and there was no Internet or home computers for many decades. So, playing board games and reading were more usual family activities, and if you wanted to talk to someone else you wrote to them or went to visit.

An Unusual Family

Children were encouraged to play outside in the fresh air when Stephen was young. Kicking footballs around didn't appeal to him, but he did enjoy playing at the bombsite on his road with his friend, Howard. The two boys spent hours carefully examining the craters that resulted from a bomb drop a few years before.

Howard lived only three doors away from Stephen, but their families were very different.

Howard's parents weren't intellectuals (people who read a lot and discuss big ideas) and they didn't listen to opera on the radio like the other adults Stephen knew. Howard's family wasn't wealthy and he didn't go to a private school like Stephen. Instead of absorbing ideas about science and politics at home, Howard had learnt all about boxing and football. It was the first time that Stephen became aware that his family was unusual.

In fact, the Hawking family was very unusual. They would probably have been called eccentric, as their lives and values were very different to most of the people around them. At a time when almost everyone was religious, they enjoyed long discussions about whether or not God existed. Stephen's father didn't drive a family car; he owned a series of old black London taxicabs.

Instead of a pet dog or cat, the Hawking family had a beehive in the basement. And while most parents told their children never to play with fire, Stephen's dad encouraged a scientific spirit by teaching his children to make fireworks in the greenhouse!

But although everyone in his family loved to talk and argue, the Hawkings were great readers and would often spend family dinners in complete silence, with their noses in their books.

FAMILY HOLIDAYS

For their holidays the Hawkings bought a large, wooden, brightly painted Roma caravan

which they kept on a site on the south coast of England. Every year they went there, taking along a large army tent to sleep in. The other holidaymakers thought the caravan was odd and asked them to remove it, but Stephen's father refused. Eventually, in 1958, the council took the caravan away.

STEPHEN'S UNIVERSE EXPANDS

At most schools in the 1950s, children learnt their lessons by rote – repeating facts until they stuck. Punishments, such as being hit on the hand with a wooden cane, were common for things as small as being late or bad-mannered. But at Byron House, Stephen's first school, the children were treated respectfully and allowed to learn at their own speed. This sounds like a better alternative, but under these methods Stephen didn't learn to read until he was eight.

Leaving London

Stephen stayed at Byron House School until his father's job moved to Mill Hill in north-west London. The family decided to leave London for a much quieter city not far away – St Albans.

There, Stephen and his sisters joined St Albans High School for Girls, which, confusingly, wasn't a high school and wasn't just for girls! They allowed boys to attend until the age of ten. Stephen wasn't there for long because around that time his mother took the children to stay with friends in Spain, while his father was away on a research trip in Africa. By the time they returned to England, Stephen was too old for the school, so he took an entrance exam for the historic St Albans School.

Stephen passed the exam, but once there he failed to impress the teachers. His handwriting was messy, he had a lot of absences because of illness and he didn't really like doing homework. Because of this, his grades were pretty average. Later, Stephen joked that this was because everyone else in his class was unusually clever. But in truth, Stephen was lazy. He had realized that because he was able to understand the maths and science more easily than his classmates, he could sit back and relax. It wasn't that he didn't like these subjects; he just didn't find the way that they were taught very interesting. However, when his mother took Stephen and his sisters to the Science Museum, Stephen found learning about science fascinating.

At St Albans School, his friends had noticed how clever Stephen was. Despite his average grades, his classmates gave him the nickname "Einstein", after one of the world's most famous scientists, Albert Einstein.

ALBERT EINSTEIN

German scientist Albert Einstein is most famous for developing the equation $E = mc^2$. This basically means that energy and matter are different forms of the same thing. He is also famous for his bushy moustache and eccentric personality!

A World of Maths

As well as being clever, Stephen was very friendly, and at school he had six or seven close friends. They talked and argued about everything, including his growing obsession: the origin of the universe and whether it developed naturally or was created by the hand of God.

At home, Stephen's father had been encouraging his interest in science and coaching him in mathematics, but this had to stop when Stephen knew more than his father.

Luckily, at just the right time, Stephen met his inspirational maths teacher, Mr Tahta, who showed him how to harness his energy and think creatively. A world of maths as the blueprint to the universe opened up to teenage Stephen, giving him the tools that would become the key to all of his great theories and discoveries. Stephen enjoyed learning with Mr Tahta so much that he began to consider studying maths at university.

His father, however, said that this was a terrible idea because he thought that the only job for a mathematician would be as a teacher. Frank continued to encourage Stephen to study the sciences, hoping that Stephen would follow in his footsteps by studying medicine. But Stephen had no interest in biology, seeing it as a science that just described what could be seen, rather than looking at how or why something works, or where it all comes from. At his school the students saw biology as an easier subject, while the cleverer boys studied physics. But Stephen didn't like physics much either, saying that it was the most boring subject at school because it was so easy and obvious. Chemistry was more fun because unexpected things happened, such as explosions. But in the end, it was physics and then astronomy that offered Stephen the chance to understand more about where humans came from and why we are here.

FUN FACTS

- The Hawking children sometimes talked so fast that they would make up words. Friends called the way they spoke 'Hawkingese'.

- Stephen had an imaginary house in a place he called 'Drane'. He was so determined to visit it that his mother worried he would try to get himself there by bus!

- When he was twelve years old, one of Stephen's classmates bet a bag of sweets that Stephen would never do well in life. Whoops!

DARING TO DREAM

A Homemade Computer

When Stephen's father was carrying out research on tropical diseases, he used to take Stephen to his laboratory at Mill Hill. Stephen loved to look through the microscopes. However, he was uncomfortable when his father took him into the insect house where they kept insects infected with tropical diseases, because there always seemed to be a few escaped ones flying around. He didn't want to get bitten and develop a tropical disease!

He still loved to take things apart to see how they worked, but he often couldn't put them back together again. He said later that he thought he learnt more than a child would today by physically doing it rather than looking on a mobile phone. However, he admitted that his practical ability was low compared to his theoretical qualities, by which he meant that he was better at analysing and dreaming up solutions than making anything with his own hands.

STEPHEN SAID...

If you understand how something works then you can control it. As he grew up he no longer destroyed toy trains in the interest of science; instead he tried to figure out the universe by applying the laws of physics.

Stephen had moved on from building model trains and boats to computers. With help from his maths teacher, Stephen and his friends built a computer from unwanted bits and pieces, such as clock parts and telephone switchboards. The boys named the finished computer the Logical Uniselector Computing Engine, known as

LUCE for short, and it made them famous at school. According to the school newspaper, it could solve some useless though quite complex logical problems. If the LUCE existed today it would undoubtedly be in a museum or auctioned for a lot of money, but sadly it was thrown away after Stephen left the school!

By his teenage years, Stephen was thinking beyond his own projects. He was alert to information that could explain the whole universe to him, so when, aged fifteen, he learnt that someone called Edwin Hubble (who the Hubble Space Telescope would be named after) had discovered that the universe is expanding, he paid attention.

THE HUBBLE SPACE TELESCOPE

Hubble is a satellite telescope positioned in space, which has given us the first clear pictures of our galaxy and beyond. Our atmosphere clouds images of space. By placing

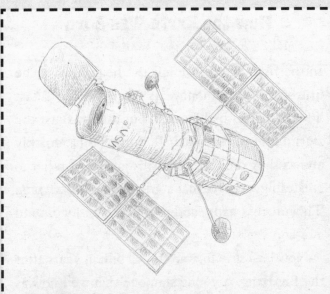

Hubble above our atmosphere, the pictures are much clearer. Although it had a few teething problems, and was initially declared a failure, it has now provided us with amazing photographs and has contributed to many discoveries. It has even helped scientists figure out the age of the universe:

13.8 BILLION YEARS OLD!

How the Earth Was Born

In the first chapter we left the beginning of the universe 400 million years after the Big Bang. The first stars had formed, but that was just the start. These "protostars" burned out quickly and as they died their centres joined together to create bigger stars that started to shine brightly. This process happened over and over for around a billion years.

Now let's skip forward to 9.2 billion years after the Big Bang. A young star, one that we know as the Sun, took shape from a large cloud of gas and dust and it

IGNITED!

Surrounding the Sun was a large disk of dust and gas made from the leftovers of dead stars. Out of this disk the planets in our solar system slowly began to appear; first Uranus, Neptune and the dwarf planet Pluto, then Jupiter, Saturn, Mercury and Venus, and last of all, Earth and Mars. And then, 9.3 billion years after the Big Bang, a massive asteroid struck the new Earth, and gravity pulled asteroid and Earth material together to form the Moon.

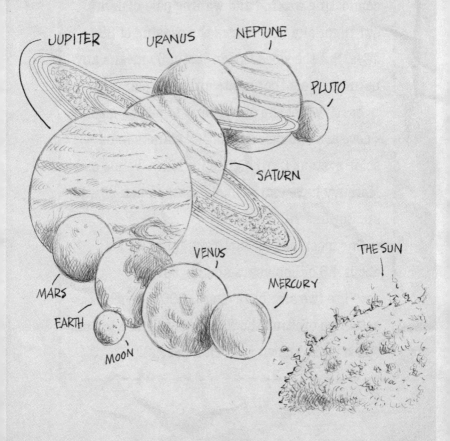

Fast forward less than a billion years and the conditions were finally right for life to begin on Earth.

WHAT EXACTLY IS A MOON?

We are used to talking about our Moon, the comforting waxing and waning pale disk in our night sky that marks the passing of 28 days. But the word "moon" actually means any natural object that orbits around a planet.

Earth is not the only planet to have a moon. There are 193 moons orbiting planets in our solar system. Our neighbours Mars, Venus and Mercury have two each, but Saturn has 62 and Jupiter has 79!

Our moon has lit Earth's night skies for about 4.5 billion years and it's our only natural satellite (we also have over 2,000 man-made satellites orbiting the Earth as well as a ton of space junk, known as orbital debris).

The Moon was formed 4.5 billion years ago when a large object hit the Earth and blasted out rocks that melted together, cooled down and orbited round the Earth. Then, for another 500 million years, pieces of rock kept crashing into the surface of the Moon. We can see the scars and craters they left today just by looking through binoculars.

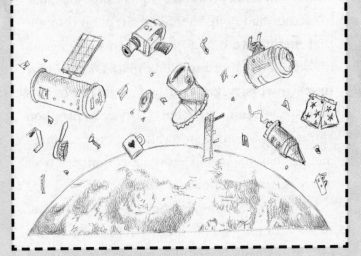

STUDYING THE UNIVERSE

Although Stephen was not a top student, he agreed with his father that he should try to go to Oxford or Cambridge University. Perhaps with his average grades in mind, he chose University College in Oxford, because his father had gone there and Stephen thought that might give him a better chance of getting in. Stephen wanted to study maths, but at that time University College had no mathematics fellow (a senior teacher). Instead Stephen applied for a course in natural sciences, which meant that he would study a combination of many different aspects of science.

However, Stephen's family was not rich, so in order to go he needed the university to award him a scholarship. This seemed unlikely, especially as Stephen was only seventeen. His school headteacher advised him to wait a year, but instead, for the first time in his life Stephen studied really hard and finally took the scholarship exam with two other boys from the year above him at school.

At the time his family was away in India for a year, but Stephen stayed behind with a family friend to study, enjoying visits to his family during the holidays. He found India very interesting but was hugely disappointed that his father refused to eat any Indian food, and had hired an ex-British army cook so that the family could continue to eat their normal English meals.

Back at home, Stephen's hard work paid off. He received a telegram saying that not only had he got in to Oxford, he had won a scholarship. Stephen had achieved an almost perfect score on the physics part of the entrance exam. On top of this, one of the professors was impressed with his humour and charm. And so in 1959, at only seventeen years old, he arrived at Oxford University.

Lazy and Cool

You might think that once he was there, Stephen would make the most of his time at university. However, he found his first year very lonely and boring. At that time at Oxford, working hard was seen as very uncool. Stephen once explained that you were supposed to be brilliant without putting any effort in, or accept that you were not brilliant and get a very bad degree. The worst thing possible was to be seen as a "grey man", a dull person whose achievements came from hard work. Stephen decided that he did not want to be a grey man, so would be lazy and cool, and as a result did very little, often skipping classes and only working for an hour a day. This didn't matter too much for the first two years, as there were no exams to pass. In fact, with only one test to sit at the end of the third year, he couldn't see the point in studying or even in going to lectures every day.

OXBRIDGE

"Oxbridge" is the name used to refer to Oxford and Cambridge universities. They are the oldest universities in Britain (Oxford is over 900 years old!) and are often seen as the very best in the world. Out of the 56 prime ministers of England, 42 attended Oxford or Cambridge.

In theory, anyone can study at Oxbridge if they get good enough grades at their A-level exams. However, these universities still take a lot of students who have been to private schools and not very many who are from different ethnic backgrounds, which can put some students off. People are trying to change this but it's very slow. Recently, Stormzy, a British rapper, launched a scholarship scheme for students of Afro-Caribbean heritage to attend Cambridge University.

Instead of studying, Stephen read science fiction books, listened to music and grew his hair long, which was the fashion at the time.

But he wasn't really having fun. Friendships were difficult for him – he had been a friendly child but was a shy teenager. Most of the other students were much older and had been in the army before coming to university. So, in order to make friends Stephen tried out for the rowing team. Oxford and Cambridge both have beautiful rivers that flow through the cities, and it's traditional for students to learn to row. Stephen was definitely not sporty and he didn't have the strong back needed to move the oars through the water, so instead he became a coxswain. This involved him sitting in the stern of the boat and steering, acting as the eyes for the rowers who faced backwards, and shouting instructions like a coach. Although he was never an athlete, Stephen earned a reputation for being daring as he guided his boat through tricky waters.

A Gamble

By the summer of 1962, Stephen's final exams loomed. The idea was that he should show what he had learnt; however, he hadn't worked very much, so he had a problem. To solve it, Stephen decided that he would leave all the questions that required him to have learnt facts blank, and just answer those that allowed him to think and write about the problems in a theoretical way.

Stephen didn't sleep well the night before the exam, and he didn't do as well as he had hoped. He wanted to get the top mark, a "first-class degree". But when the results came through,

Stephen was on the borderline between a first- and a second-class degree, so the examiners asked him to come for an interview to help them decide which grade to give him.

Stephen knew that he was in trouble if they wanted him to prove that he had learnt all of his coursework. So, he took a gamble that the university would only want to keep really exceptional students. When the examiners asked Stephen about his future plans he replied that he wanted to continue studying at Oxford. He then said that if they awarded him a first-class degree, he would leave Oxford and go to Cambridge. If they gave him a second-class degree (a lower grade) he would stay at Oxford to continue his studies.

The examiners gave him a first. Stephen would joke that they did this to get rid of him because he had been such a bad student, but in fact his tutor Robert Berman has said that the examiners realized that they were talking to someone far cleverer than themselves, and this is why they awarded him the highest degree possible.

Life at Cambridge

In 1962, when he was still only twenty years old, Stephen Hawking arrived at the Department of Applied Mathematics and Theoretical Physics at Cambridge University to begin his research degree.

WHAT IS A RESEARCH DEGREE?

A research degree is also known as a PhD (a Doctorate of Philosophy). It is a very unusual qualification because you're not taught anything new – you discover it yourself. This is why it's called a research degree!

In fact, in order to pass you have to find and show something important and new about the subject you're studying, and then write your discovery up into a book called a "thesis", which is read by examiners to decide if you should pass or not. When you have gained a PhD you become a "doctor" (but not a medical one!). Sometimes people who complete PhDs go on to work at a university as a research fellow, where they continue their own work or help others with their studies.

Stephen had hoped that at Cambridge he would work with a famous scientist, Fred Hoyle. Stephen was upset to find out, however, that Fred Hoyle was a very popular choice with research students. Instead, Stephen's supervisor was Dennis Sciama – a man he had never heard of.

Later in life, Stephen said he was very pleased that he didn't end up with Dennis, because although Dennis was the person who came up with the name Big Bang, he meant it as an insult to a theory he didn't believe in. As his student, Stephen would have been drawn into the impossible task of defending Dennis' alternative belief to the Big Bang theory, the "steady-state theory". Sciama, however, was a leading cosmologist, and over the years he helped Stephen to form many of his famous theories, including the subject of Stephen's PhD thesis.

ASTRONOMY VS COSMOLOGY

Astronomy is the study of stars, galaxies and everything in space.

Cosmology is the study of the universe as a whole, including how it began, how it grew and how it will end.

STEADY-STATE THEORY

The steady-state theory says that the universe has no beginning or end. It explains the fact that the universe is expanding by suggesting that new matter is constantly created to fill the space. This theory is no longer believed.

The Big Bang Theory

Stephen had been thinking about the expanding universe since he was fifteen. At the time most scientists believed in the steady-state theory. This didn't make sense to Stephen because it meant that the universe didn't begin and couldn't end. Stephen thought instead that the universe was expanding like a balloon – it had a beginning and there would come a point where it would end.

Stephen wrote his thesis in 1966. It was titled "Properties of Expanding Universes", and it proved how the Big Bang theory (the universe beginning from a single point and then expanding out in all directions) was physically possible. He had shown that the steady-state model, that people had believed until that point, was wrong.

STEPHEN SAID...

After his PhD thesis was posted online years later, Stephen said that if anyone didn't like it, instead of complaining directly to him they should contact his younger self. He then added they would have to invent time travel to do so!

Maths!

It's hard for most of us to understand how Stephen could work out something as crazily complicated as how the universe began. But the answer is quite simply – he used maths! Galileo, one of Stephen's greatest heroes, said that our universe is a grand book written in the language of mathematics.

Maths isn't just about numbers – it's about patterns and shapes. This is particularly useful in cosmology, for working out the trajectories (patterns) of moving objects: their orbits. Scientists noticed that just as an object you throw follows the same shape (an upside-down parabola, or flattened U shape), the way that things move in orbit in space also follows a shape. This shape is an ellipse (like a rugby ball), which is related to a parabola.

Humans have discovered shapes that repeat in all areas of nature, and this is within what we call the laws of physics. In the same way that the laws that make up our legal system are written in words, the laws of physics are written in maths.

So, because our whole universe is mathematical, scientists can use maths to tell us about incredible events that happened in the past, even 13.8 billion years ago!

LAWS OF PHYSICS

A law of physics is a fact that scientists have understood and agreed about the physical world. Many of these laws we take for granted – for example, we laugh at a cartoon character who walks off a cliff but doesn't fall straight away, because we understand basic laws of universal gravitation.

From a combination of observations and knowledge of the laws of physics, scientists can design telescopes, satellites and space rockets and make predictions about parts of the universe we can't reach or even see.

DIZZYING FACT

The universe is expanding fast. A galaxy 3.26 million light years from us is moving away at 71 kilometres (44 miles) a second. However, the further away something is from us, the faster it moves. So a galaxy 326 million light years away is moving at an astonishing 7,100 kilometres (4,411 miles) per second!

EVERY DAY'S A BONUS

Outside of his studies, Stephen's life was not going well.

In his last year at Oxford, Stephen had noticed that he was getting clumsy. He fell over once or twice for no apparent reason, and he could no longer row. And then, while he was working on his thesis, Stephen's speech became slurred and he often dropped things. He knew something was wrong, so he went to see a doctor. But he was told not to worry and that it was just the effects of drinking too much beer.

Back at home for the Christmas holidays, Stephen agreed to go ice-skating with his family, though he knew he didn't feel well enough. While skating Stephen fell over and couldn't get up again. Stephen's mother finally realized that something was very wrong and she took him to another doctor.

Stephen spent a terrifying week having tests at St Bartholomew's Hospital in London. A tiny piece of muscle was taken from his arm to be tested. Then he had electrodes attached (small needles with wires that were connected to a machine) while fluid was injected into his spine. He was tilted on his bed as doctors watched the liquid moving up and down on X-ray machines.

Strangely, for someone so curious, Stephen didn't ask what was wrong with him and the doctors didn't tell him. But he guessed enough to know that whatever he had was serious and that it would only get worse.

Once the doctors had their results they informed him that they could do nothing for him. They gave him vitamins and sent him home.

Things looked terrible for Stephen. But while he had been in hospital there had been a boy he knew in the bed opposite him, who had leukaemia (cancer of the blood). Sadly, the boy had died. At that point Stephen realized that although he was ill, at least he didn't feel it. So, whenever he felt sorry for himself he thought of that boy and knew that things could be worse.

By now Stephen's mother had consulted with doctors and found out what was causing Stephen's coordination problems. He had developed a disease called amyotrophic lateral sclerosis (also known as ALS), in which the nerve cells of the brain and spinal cord waste away and then scar or go hard.

Stephen's doctors had said that he wasn't a typical case, but they predicted that he only had two years left to live. Stephen was twenty-one years old. It was hard for him to accept that his life was going to be so short.

WHAT DOES "ALS" MEAN?

ALS stands for "amyotrophic lateral sclerosis". This complicated name comes from the Greek language. If we break it down, we can see its meaning:

A-myo-trophic:
"A" means no

"Myo" refers to muscle

"Trophic" means nourishment

So, together they mean **"no muscle nourishment"** – that a muscle is starved.

"Lateral" refers to the place on the spinal cord where the damage happens, and **"sclerosis"** means hardening.

ALS is also known as Lou Gehrig's disease, after a famous American baseball star who died of the disease. In Britain, it is usually called motor neurone disease or MND.

WHY IS ALS SO SERIOUS?

The disease attacks the nerves that control muscle function, making the person unable to walk, talk or make any voluntary movements. The disease gets worse as time goes on. Involuntary muscles, like the heart, continue to work normally, but it makes the body very weak so that patients can't fight off other diseases.

At first Stephen got worse very quickly. He was losing the use of his body fast, and he was depressed. At one point, working seemed pointless because he didn't know if he would even live long enough to finish the PhD that he had started.

But then, fortunately, Stephen's condition stabilized. He stopped weakening as fast and felt more enthusiastic about his studies. Suddenly, Stephen began to appreciate what he had.

EVERY DAY WAS A BONUS.

He said later that before he became ill he had been bored with his life and didn't think that there was anything worth doing. But he then realized that there was a lot he wanted to do with whatever time he had left.

RECORD-BREAKING STEPHEN!

Most people only live for about three years from when ALS is first noticed, and only five per cent live longer than 20 years with the disease. But Stephen lived for 55 years after his diagnosis.

The chief scientist of the ALS Association in America has said that she didn't know of anyone who survived ALS longer than Stephen.

LOVE, FAME AND SUCCESS

He might have felt that his world was ending, but wonderful things awaited Stephen.

At the beginning of the autumn term at Cambridge, Stephen had moved into new student rooms. He didn't know anyone yet, so he went to a party hoping to make some friends. He dressed up in a black velvet jacket and a red velvet bow tie and, although normally Stephen was shy around girls, he began to chat to Jane Wilde, a friend of his sister, making her laugh with the story of how he had managed to get a first by threatening to stay at Oxford if they gave him a second-class degree. Jane thought he seemed arrogant but intelligent, although she didn't then know what cosmology was. But mostly she found Stephen interesting and she liked the way he could laugh at himself. It turned out that they had a lot in common.

Jane had grown up living close to Stephen in St Albans, and the two had even gone to the same school, though Jane was a few years younger so they hadn't known each other. Jane was also academic and ambitious, but her speciality was languages, not science like Stephen. Although they had grown up near to each other, Jane and Stephen came from very different worlds. Stephen's family didn't believe in God and were more interested in talking about science and art, while Jane's family were religious and very traditional. But the two liked each other at once and before they left the party they exchanged addresses.

Stephen and Jane started seeing each other regularly but Stephen kept his illness a secret. Eventually, Stephen had to face up to both the disease and his love for Jane and he asked her to marry him. Although she knew that Stephen was ill and would one day be unable to move his body, she agreed.

It was Jane, and his studies, that became Stephen's focus. Jane told him that together they would fight his condition and this gave Stephen something to live for. Stephen and Jane were married on 14 July 1965, when Stephen was twenty-three and Jane was twenty-one. They were full of hope for the future.

Black Holes

Now that he had a focus, Stephen didn't complain about his illness, even though he could no longer move as well as before. Writing down his calculations started to become difficult, so he developed a way of imagining maths so that he could see the problems in his head.

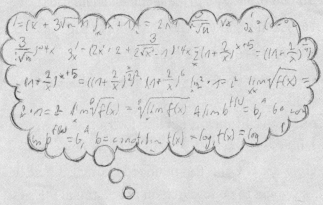

Jane was happy to type Stephen's work up for him and this unusual method of working was so successful that a year after they married, Stephen came equal first place in an important award – the Adams Prize – where he had submitted work on black holes. Also, in 1966, Stephen finally finished and passed his PhD.

ADAMS PRIZE

The Adams Prize is one of Cambridge University's most important awards. It began in 1848 to celebrate mathematician John Couch Adams, who discovered the planet Neptune after studying why Uranus had such an odd orbit. The prize is for mathematical researchers under the age of forty and winners are given a cash prize.

Stephen had already applied for a job as a research fellow at another Cambridge college called Gonville & Caius (pronounced "keys"). There he was going to do research on gravitational physics.

GRAVITY

We all need gravity! Gravity is a force that draws objects towards each other. All objects have it, but the more mass an object has, the more gravity it produces. The Earth has a huge mass and a lot of gravity, which is why we don't float out of bed and when we put down a cup it stays there. But the Sun's gravity is even stronger, so it holds us and the other planets in our solar system in its orbit.

DID YOU KNOW?

The Earth's gravitational pull keeps the sea in place, but the Moon's pull is strong enough to make the oceans bulge slightly, which is why we have tides.

A Breakthrough

It usually takes a long time for a research scientist to make a breakthrough but in 1974, when Stephen Hawking was still only thirty-two, he published a discovery that changed the way that science thinks about black holes. Scientists don't work alone and Stephen's first important contribution to cosmology came after working for many years with another famous scientist, Roger Penrose. Their results showed that during the Big Bang, the universe began in a singularity – these results became known as the Penrose–Hawking singularity theorems. 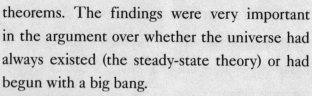 The findings were very important in the argument over whether the universe had always existed (the steady-state theory) or had begun with a big bang.

At first it looked like Stephen's breakthrough was going to be ignored by the scientific community. Then the science journal, *Nature* – a magazine that prints all kinds of important essays on science – decided to ignore the disbelievers and publish the paper.

The change in Stephen's life was immediate. Suddenly, people from all over the world had heard of Stephen Hawking and his theory about radiation escaping from black holes. He began to be seen as a very important scientist.

Stephen's discovery and brilliance was made official when he was elected to the Royal Society, which was the first ever society for science, and over 350 years old. Stephen had now earned the respect of the scientific community.

THEORY OR THEOREM?

They sound similar, but are in fact different!

Theory is a set of ideas used to explain why something is true.

Theorem is a result that can be shown to be true.

WORKING TOGETHER

Stephen was not only influenced by great scientists from the past – people living and working at the same time as him were vital to his work, too. It was thanks to the work of Roger Penrose that Stephen made the biggest breakthroughs of his career. Roger was the son of a psychiatrist and mathematician. Early on in his career he became interested in impossible shapes and, with his father, invented the Penrose stairs

Later he revolutionized the mathematical tools that were use to understand space-time and helped Stephen with his first breakthrough.

Stephen later became lifelong friends with other famous scientists, Richard Feynman and Kip Thorne, who he met when he and his young family spent a year at the California Institute of Technology (Caltech) in America. The three didn't just enjoy working together, they also liked to joke around and make bets about unproven scientific theories.

Now that Stephen was a famous scientist he loved to get involved in arguments with his scientific friends and colleagues about new theories and would place bets on the results. One of his most famous wagers was that the Higgs boson particle would never be found. Understandably, Peter Higgs, who believed he had proved its existence in 1964, was not happy about this. They had big debates about it in public, where Higgs criticized Stephen's work and claimed that people only listened to him because he was now a celebrity. Unfortunately for Stephen, the Higgs boson was discovered in 2012 following the building of the Large Hadron Collider. Stephen was quick to announce that he had lost his bet, and even suggested that Higgs should win the Nobel Prize for Physics, which he did the following year.

THE HIGGS BOSON

The Higgs boson is a particle that gives mass to other particles. It's sometimes known as the "God particle" because it's so important to physics that without it the world couldn't exist. However big it may be in importance, it's so small that it took over forty years for scientists to find it, which they did using the Large Hadron Collider.

THE LARGE HADRON COLLIDER

> The Large Hadron Collider whizzes particles of atoms down a 27-kilometre long tunnel (16.8 miles) at nearly the speed of light, letting them crash into each other to recreate how things were just after the Big Bang.

Without Roger Penrose, Stephen's big breakthrough could not have happened. Thanks to Penrose's interest in black holes, Stephen decided in 1971 to research black holes because not much was known about them.

Black Holes

Black holes are an area of space where gravity pulls everything that reaches its rim (known as the "event horizon") inside – even light! Which is why we can't see a black hole. We only know it's there because of what it has swallowed up.

Two years into his research, Stephen was puzzled by some of his calculations. He made sure the maths was correct, and then he realized that what his numbers were telling him was hugely important because it reversed how scientists had thought that black holes worked. The belief was that nothing could escape, but Stephen was sure he had seen particles and energy streaming out of a black hole and into space!

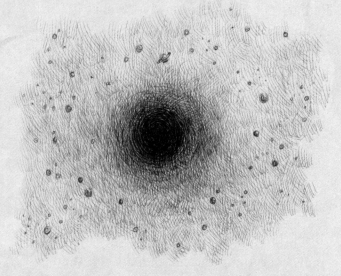

He realized that if a small amount of radiation and energy could emerge from a black hole, then the hole would slowly shrink. And as it shrunk it would get hotter. According to his calculations it would shrink down so far that in the end it would evaporate.

But this would happen so slowly that there was no chance of anyone witnessing it, and at first, when Stephen spoke to other scientists about it, no one believed him.

RADIATION

Radiation is the name we give to energy moving from one place to another in waves or particles. Light, sound, heat and X-rays are all types of radiation.

HAWKING RADIATION

First, we need to understand that pairs of particles are constantly popping into existence in space. It's weird but true. It gets stranger as the two parts – the particle and antiparticle – immediately cancel each other out. This happens so fast that normally we don't see either the particle or antiparticle of these pairs. But if a pair suddenly appears right at the event horizon of a black hole, one of the pair may be sucked inside while the other remains outside. The one that has gone inside will then pair up with another particle, which will very slightly reduce the mass and energy inside the black hole.

The Hawking Paradox

Much later, Stephen was forced to look again at his research into black holes. Ever since he had first published his theory, scientists had argued over it. They had even given the problem a name: the "black hole information paradox" or simply, the "Hawking Paradox". The issue was that Stephen claimed black holes released subatomic particles, (known as Hawking radiation) until they evaporate. However, this is against the laws of physics that state that particles can't be created or destroyed.

Stephen defended his theory until 2004, when some Russian scientists proved his maths wrong. So, he changed his mind! Stephen suggested that what came back out of a black hole was like a burned book – it was still there but would be impossible to read.

The Hawking Paradox is still being researched but Stephen was happy to concede that he had been wrong. However, in 2016, Professor Jeff Steinhauer of the Technion university in Israel was able to test the concept of Hawking Radiation by creating a tiny black hole made of sound waves. Other scientists are now scrambling to try this out themselves, but it looks possible that Stephen's theory, based on mathematics, could soon be proven in the lab!

WHAT IS THE MILKY WAY?

The Milky Way is the name of the galaxy we live in. It's formed in the shape of a spiral, and is about 100,000 light years across. It's called the Milky Way because it looks like a glowing milky band stretching across the night sky.

MILKY WAY

SUPERMASSIVE BLACK HOLES

You may remember from the first chapter that black holes are the most destructive things in the universe – and if you are unlucky enough to fall inside one you will become spaghettified!

But some black holes are more destructive than others. The largest ones are called "supermassive". Supermassive black holes are the oldest ones and weigh as much as 4,000,000 suns!

There are a few million small black holes in the Milky Way, and one supermassive black hole in the centre. Scientists believe there is a supermassive black hole at the centre of every galaxy.

WE ARE ALL DIFFERENT

While Stephen's family was growing and his career was advancing, his symptoms were worsening. He walked using canes and crutches for a few years, but then, in 1969, he had lost the strength in his legs and settled on using a wheelchair.

Life was very frustrating for Jane. She still hadn't finished her education and was also typing up Stephen's research papers because he could no longer use a typewriter. While Stephen was able to work on scientific theories, and loved to play outside with the children, he was unable to help with the washing-up or making meals. Jane wanted to remain positive but she was frustrated and exhausted and tried to persuade Stephen that they needed someone to help them.

It wasn't until 1974 that Stephen agreed to allow a graduate student to live with the family to help Jane take care of him and the children. The student they chose was called Bernard Carr and he went on to become a professor of mathematics and astronomy, so he fitted in well in the household. After that, Stephen became used to having help, which improved life for the whole family.

STEPHEN'S CHILDREN

Robert

Stephen's eldest son Robert was a serious child, and the only one who showed an interest in science. Robert decided to study computing, and after attending Oxford University like his father, he became a well-known software engineer.

Lucy

Stephen's only daughter, Lucy, only realized that her dad was very ill when she was seven. She too attended Oxford, studying languages, and became a journalist and author, writing a series of books for children with her father about space and science.

Tim

Stephen's youngest son, Tim, couldn't understand his father until he got his synthesized voice when Tim was five, but the pair

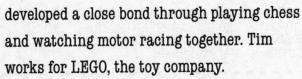

developed a close bond through playing chess and watching motor racing together. Tim works for LEGO, the toy company.

Grandchildren

Stephen had three grandchildren. Two live in the USA with their father, Robert. Lucy's son, William, lives in England and was very close to Stephen. He has autism and when Stephen won the Special Breakthrough Prize in Fundamental Physics for a lifetime of achievements, he decided that he would use some of the money to help William.

Fun family facts

Stephen was very competitive when he played chess with his children.

Tim loved to reprogram his father's synthesized voice to say rude words!

Stephen was usually a relaxed dad, but he didn't allow his children to watch the music programme *Top of the Pops*.

Equal Opportunity

In 1977, Stephen was given the title of Professor Hawking, in the gravitational physics department of Cambridge University. This meant that he was now helping students who were studying for a PhD, the same qualification he had been studying for only recently. It also meant that he would have more time for his own research and theories. Although now a professor, he was still frustrated at how difficult it was for him as a disabled person to move around both at the university and in the outside world. Even Stephen's parents didn't really take into account his disability when they bought a house at the top of a steep hill!

Cambridge University had begun to adapt their buildings for wheelchair users, installing ramps and disabled parking, but in order for Stephen to be independent it still wasn't enough. It was then that Stephen began campaigning to improve the lives of other disabled people.

Jane helped by writing letters to the

government asking for more to be done to help disabled people, and Stephen began to argue publicly for equal rights for all. Governments had a moral duty, he told them. Not only should Cambridge University change to make access possible for disabled people, but so should all public buildings and schools, otherwise there wasn't an equal opportunity for everyone to work or to learn.

You Can Achieve Anything

Daily life was a struggle, but there were exciting times for Stephen, too. As Stephen's career became ever more successful, he was invited to conferences in the USA. All of the Hawking family went along, and Stephen's disability made him very noticeable. The way he appeared to overcome his problems, combined with his brilliance and success, was inspirational to everyone he met.

Stephen knew that he was lucky in some ways, and, importantly that he was in a unique position to demand change. He wasn't seen as just another person with a disability, he was a genius and people saw past his disability. In addition to arguing that change was needed in terms of architecture, Stephen also wanted to alter how others viewed people like him. He liked to be able to show that someone in a wheelchair was still capable of achieving amazing things.

Stephen thought it was important to speak directly to people with all types of disabilities. He often met with children, especially those in wheelchairs, so that he could show them what the man who was given two years to live had achieved. He said that he had learnt from his disability to focus on the things he could do, not the things he couldn't – his disability hadn't been a serious handicap in his work. He wanted to encourage people to realize their full potential, as he had.

Future Stephen

In 2001, when he was much older, Stephen made a TV show where he tried out new technology for people with disabilities. These innovations have also helped to develop technologies that many of us take for granted today, such as Siri, Alexa and other voice activated technology. Sadly, many people who have conditions such as MND/ALS do not have access to the communication technology that would help their independence.

Stephen spoke to the world when he appeared on stage at the London Paralympics opening ceremony in 2012, narrating a piece based on Shakespeare's *The Tempest*, where a character, Miranda, goes on a journey of discovery around the themes of reason and human rights. He was delighted to be there and said he wanted to show the world that, no matter the differences between people, it's important to remember that everyone is good at something.

STEPHEN SAID...

"WE ARE ALL DIFFERENT. THERE IS NO SUCH THING AS A STANDARD OR RUN-OF-THE-MILL HUMAN BEING."

EQUALIZER

Stephen had walked with the help of sticks and crutches since soon after his diagnosis. He put off using a wheelchair for as long as he could, but once it was necessary, he also got himself a blue electric three-wheeled car, which travelled at the speed of slow cycling – and in which he liked to illegally carry passengers!

Stephen loved the independence that his first electric wheelchair gave him. He was often seen whizzing around Cambridge and was said to run over the toes of people who annoyed him. He even once ran over the toes of Prince Charles, though that was apparently an accident!

Robert, Lucy and Tim loved to ride on their dad's wheelchair, and he would chase them around in it, too. Lucy said that at the time it was unusual to see someone out and about in a wheelchair and she hated her family being stared at. But her friends accepted it easily and were particularly impressed to see the skill with which Stephen could spin in circles!

STEPHEN SAID...

"REMEMBER TO LOOK UP AT THE STARS AND NOT DOWN AT YOUR FEET."

A Turn for the Worse

By the early 1980s, Stephen's speech was being affected by his ALS. It had been becoming gradually more slurred so only people who knew him well could understand him. Even Stephen's youngest son, Tim, couldn't really follow what he said. People would ask Stephen's children, Lucy and Robert, to translate for him. Lucy said they became very good at understanding the facial twitches that meant yes and no, and he would secretly message to them when he wanted to leave somewhere and they would make a fast exit.

Thankfully, Stephen was still able to write his papers. He had a secretary he would dictate to, and when he taught his students he had an interpreter who could understand him and repeat his words.

But in 1985, Stephen's health took a bad turn. He was in Switzerland on a work trip with other scientists when he became ill with pneumonia, a severe lung infection. As his muscles got even weaker he began to choke. By the time Jane had flown to his side he was being helped to breathe by a ventilator machine. Seeing how terribly ill and weak Stephen was, doctors told Jane that there was nothing they could do to save her husband and asked for her permission to turn off the machine.

However, Jane was convinced that if she could get Stephen home he would get better. Luckily, doctors at Addenbrooke's Hospital in Cambridge knew how to save Stephen's life, but it came at a terrible price. They would have to fit a special breathing tube to his neck to let air in. Stephen would never be able to speak again.

Stephen survived and gradually recovered, but when he was well enough to go home, apart from being unable to speak, he could not feed himself or even get out of bed without help. The time had come when he was going to need full-time care. The family were faced with a choice – Stephen could go into a care home and be looked after there or they could pay privately for nurses to live with them and take care of Stephen's physical needs.

Jane absolutely refused to let Stephen be put into a nursing home to be looked after by strangers. Apart from the fact that he would hate it, they both wanted Stephen to be part of the children's lives. But this kind of care was very expensive and the family weren't rich enough to pay for it. So, Jane researched and wrote letters, and finally managed to find an American charity that would pay for Stephen's care, providing enough money for three nurses to work in shifts, so that there was always one there to give him the help he needed.

"My Name is Stephen Hawking."

Now that his life was no longer in danger, Stephen needed to find a way to communicate. At first, he and Jane tried a card system. Stephen would raise his eyebrows to choose letters from a card and spell out words. This was a very slow and frustrating way to talk, so they searched for a better method.

The better method was already out there. It was called "Equalizer" and had been made in California, USA, by a computer programmer called Walter Woltosz. He had designed Equalizer for his mother-in-law's particular needs, so when asked to make another by one of his colleagues, Walter wasn't keen. But when he was told who it was for he immediately changed his mind and said he would build it for free.

THE EQUALIZER SYSTEM

Walter's mother-in-law had ALS like Stephen, and had lost her ability to speak, though she did have movement in her fingers. Using his computer programming skills, Walter developed a system that allowed her to create sentences by using her fingers to scan and highlight words.

Because Stephen's disability was different to his mother-in-law's, Walter visited Stephen in England to work out the best way for him to operate the software. Stephen had movement in his thumb so they chose a switch method.

The software worked a lot like predictive text. The computer was programmed with 2,500 to 3,000 words and phrases that Stephen used regularly, including many very scientific terms, and Stephen could press a switch to select what he wanted to say, based on the computer producing likely choices.

When the computer was finished, Stephen's family gathered to hear his first words. "**My name is Stephen Hawking**," said the synthesized voice that the technology had given him. Everyone was surprised. He sounded like a robot with an American accent! Lucy, who was fifteen at the time, remembers everyone saying, "Oh, you're American!" But Stephen didn't care. As long as he could talk again he was happy. His five-year-old son, Tim, was happy, too – he could finally have a two-way conversation with his dad.

In this first version of his voice technology, Stephen could only talk if he was sitting next to his computer. It was frustrating not to be able to move around. So, a system was designed for an *Apple II* computer that could be attached to his wheelchair. Stephen's voice was now mobile. He could produce up to fifteen words a minute, which is slower than standard speech, but it meant Stephen could prepare his lectures in advance and his speech synthesizer could deliver them at a normal speed.

Stephen's voice became famous all over the world. No one seemed to mind that he was an English man with a robotic

American voice; it was now part of his unique image.

NEW BEGINNINGS

Unfortunately, Jane and Stephen separated in 1990. A few years later Stephen married his nurse, Elaine Mason, who he also later separated from. Jane also remarried. Despite this, Jane, Stephen and their children remained a very loving family.

Upgrade

Equalizer gave Stephen years of freedom to express himself, but eventually it became outdated and slow. Luckily, when Stephen was at a conference in 1997, the co-founder of computer company called Intel, Gordon Moore, offered to build Stephen what he called a "real computer".

They began working together to develop the

software, and from then on Stephen's computer was replaced every two years to make up for his gradually weakening muscles.

ACAT

Intel released the computer coding that made Stephen's speech system work on the Internet as "open source code". This means that the system, known as ACAT, is available for free so that other developers can use it when they are designing communication aids for people.

Stephen was offered the chance to replace the robotic American voice, but he had been using it for so long and it was so well known that he had begun to think of it as his own, and decided to keep it. He liked it so much that when the synthesizer stopped working properly Stephen bought the only three that were left in the world so he would always have spares.

Stephen copyrighted his voice to stop anyone else sounding exactly like him! When the film of his life was made he had to give permission to allow the filmmakers to use it.

Everyone was aware that, as his muscles weakened further, Stephen could lose all movement and be left with something called locked-in syndrome where he would only have eye movement. So, Stephen and the researchers tried out systems that could translate his brain patterns or facial expressions into switch activations, but these weren't successful.

Stephen was able to control his computer by the switch until 2005, when he lost movement in his thumb. To overcome this one of his graduate students developed a new system that detected his cheek movement by an infrared switch mounted on his glasses. This served him for the rest of his life.

STEPHEN'S WHEELCHAIR

Stephen had many wheelchairs throughout his life, but his final wheelchair was very special indeed. It was made by a company called BEC Mobility and at the auction where it was sold after his death, the auctioneer said that it was literally and metaphorically the most travelled wheelchair in history.

The wheelchair was expected to sell for between £10,000 and £15,000, but actually sold for almost £300,000!

AN ENDLESS UNIVERSE

In 1979, Cambridge University voted to give Stephen the biggest honour that can be awarded to a teacher of maths and science. He was made the Lucasian Professor of Mathematics. This role is also sometimes called Newton's Chair because Sir Isaac Newton, who discovered gravity, held this post nearly 300 years before Stephen.

There is a big book that every university teaching officer is asked to sign. After Stephen had been Lucasian Professor for more than a year they realized that he still hadn't signed it. They brought the book to Stephen's office – sadly, this was the last time he was ever able to sign his name.

SIR ISAAC NEWTON

Newton was a mathematician, physicist, astronomer, expert in religion and an author.

Although he died in 1727, he is still seen as one of the most important scientists ever. He is famously believed to have come up with the theory of gravity when an apple fell from a tree and hit him on the head!

He also developed the laws of motion (which formed the basis for modern physics), a branch of maths called calculus, and the reflecting telescope (a telescope in which a mirror is used to collect and focus light).

Newton once said that he had "stood on the shoulders of giants", meaning that his discoveries were only possible because of the scientists that had gone before him. Inspired by this, Stephen published a series of essays entitled *On the Shoulders of Giants* as a way of acknowledging the scientists of the past who had made his own work possible.

No End to the Universe

Despite his teaching work, young family and disability, Stephen continued his ground-breaking research, next looking at exploding black holes, the birth of black holes in our universe, and string theory. His breakthrough with Hawking Radiation had made him even more convinced of the need for one "theory of everything" that could combine general relativity and quantum theory into a theory of quantum gravity.

In the 1980s, Stephen began to question the Big Bang theory. He suggested that there had been a start to the universe, but there may be no end. Instead, there would be a constant transition of one universe becoming another through glitches in space-time.

STRING THEORY

To physicists, who study energy and matter, a string is anything much longer than it is wide.

To a mathematician a string has no width, only length.

Scientists are beginning to believe that absolutely everything, from stars to candy floss, may be made of string – very tiny, mathematical string. String theory tries to explain everything – gravity, electromagnetism, strong nuclear force, weak nuclear force – all in one.

Chaos and Facts

Although the Hawking family loved to debate and deny the existence of God, Stephen had once won a prize for religious studies (Divinity) at school. Thinking about where a divine aspect to the creation of the universe (that is, God!) fits into science became very important to Stephen in his work. Some people believed in what they called the Grand Design, based on Sir Isaac Newton's statement that the universe must have initially been made by God as it was not possible for it to have been created out of such chaos.

Stephen, in contrast, was an atheist – someone who doesn't believe in the existence of any god. He believed in scientific fact and thought that the laws of physics, not the will of God, could explain how life on Earth came into being. Some people had suggested that you could call the laws that science has worked out "God", but Stephen said this wouldn't be the sort of personal god who you could ask questions!

But Stephen had to be careful how he spoke

about God because his words might upset people who held religious beliefs. He avoided mentioning his personal beliefs in public and in his first book, *A Brief History of Time*, it seemed that he accepted that God had a role in creating the universe.

But in his 2010 book, *The Grand Design*, co-written with American physicist Leonard Mlodinow, Stephen declared that Sir Isaac Newton was wrong, and that science has now proven that a creator is not necessary in order to explain the beginnings of the universe.

Despite not believing in God, Stephen met with four different popes during his lifetime and accepted a very special Pius XI Medal for his scientific work. He was also a member of the Pontifical Academy of Sciences and helped to connect science and faith.

In 2011, Stephen said that he believed we only have one life in which to appreciate the grand design of the universe, and he was very grateful to have this opportunity.

PIUS XI MEDAL

The Pius XI Medal is awarded by the Pontifical Academy of Sciences every two years to a promising scientist who is under the age of forty-five. Stephen won the medal in 1975 for astronomy. Previous winners have included researchers in chemistry, mathematics and even geography.

A BRIEF HISTORY OF TIME

By the early 1980s, Stephen had realized that teaching his students wasn't enough. He wanted to share his knowledge about maths, black holes and the universe with the whole world. For hundreds of years scientists had come up with theories about how the universe was created. But these were all individual theories. Stephen wanted to find a unifying theory – his theory of everything – but he was no longer happy just researching it. He wanted to talk to ordinary people about the idea that there might be a single idea that provides an answer to everything in the universe.

Stephen decided to write a book. Many scientists had written on these subjects, but the difference would be that ordinary people would read Stephen's book, and it would help them to appreciate these big, hard-to-grasp ideas. He said that he wanted his book to be the type that people buy at airports, like a novel.

The Writing Process

Stephen struggled to get the ideas that would make him famous on to paper. Back then, his computer only allowed him to write fifteen words a minute, so it was going to be a slow process, but he wrote determinedly until he had a first draft ready to show to publishers. People in the industry knew that it was coming, and there were a lot of publishers who were interested in his book, but Stephen had already decided that he wanted it to go to Bantam Press because they sold a lot of books at supermarkets, American drugstores, and, of course, at airport bookshops!

Bantam Press was delighted to have the opportunity to publish a book by the genius Stephen Hawking, but when they saw it, they knew that first it needed to be entirely rewritten and all the equations had to go. Although Stephen had tried to simplify it enough for non-scientists, it was still too difficult for people who didn't understand complicated maths. So, his editor patiently worked with him, asking Stephen for explanations, until it was understood what he meant. This was the key to making a book that anyone could read.

Stephen wanted to call the book *From the Big Bang to Black Holes: A Short History of Time*, but his editor persuaded him that *A Brief History of Time* was snappier and would make more people buy it. The book was short and only contained one equation, Einstein's famous $E = mc^2$.

WHAT'S IN *A BRIEF HISTORY OF TIME*?

While it covers many subjects within cosmology, such as the Big Bang and black holes, *A Brief History of Time* also talks about space-time. One of the tricky topics that Stephen explained was that space and time are not really two different things. This feels wrong – they're *totally different* things, right? But, no. Space-time is a model that joins space and time into a single idea called a 'continuum'. It says that the rate we can see time passing depends on an object's speed in relation to the person observing it.

Space-time, Stephen explains, is like a tightly stretched sheet, and the planets are like heavy bowling balls on the sheet. Combining space and time in this way helped cosmologists to understand how the universe works on both the level of galaxies and atoms.

A Briefer History of Time

A Brief History of Time was a huge success. It was one of the most influential science books of the twentieth century. And Stephen's wish came true: it was sold at airports!

The first cover showed Stephen in a wheelchair. This image made him instantly recognizable and a very unlikely celebrity outside of the world of science. This allowed him to continue to write books and popularize cosmology, bringing science to ordinary readers all over the world.

So far, more than 10 million copies of this book have been sold and it has been translated into thirty-five languages. But for most people it is still very complicated. So, in 2005, seventeen years after this book was released, Stephen published a simpler version called *A Briefer History of Time*.

A Theory of Everything

While now a famous science writer, Stephen's mind often travelled back to earlier research. In the 1980s he was busy trying to answer the problem that had stumped Albert Einstein many years before – the 'unified field theory', or the theory of everything. He was looking for a way to describe all the fundamental forces of nature and how they react with each other in a single theory.

This one theory could explain so much, from the laws that govern nature now to how things were at the beginning of the universe. Stephen said that once humans have finally understood the unified field theory, we would know the mind of God (although as he didn't believe in

God he probably didn't mean it literally!).

In 2010, Stephen published a book with Leonard Mlodinow, *The Grand Design*, in which he described his last attempt at a theory of everything. This was his second book to hit the bestseller lists.

STEPHEN THE AUTHOR

As well as all of his academic works, Stephen wrote more than twenty books. Here are the best-known ones:

A Brief History of Time (1988)

Black Holes and Baby Universes and Other Essays (1993)

The Universe in a Nutshell (2001)

On the Shoulders of Giants (2002)

God Created the Integers (2005)

The Grand Design (with Leonard Mlodinow) (2010)

The Dreams That Stuff is Made Of (2011)

My Brief History (2013)

Brief Answers to the Big Questions (2018)

Inspired by the questions he was asked by his grandson William and his friends, Stephen wrote a series of adventure books for children together with his daughter, Lucy. The books are part adventure story and part science book:

George's Secret Key to the Universe (2007)
George's Cosmic Treasure Hunt (2009)
George and the Big Bang (2011)
George and the Unbreakable Code (2014)
George and the Blue Moon (2016)

Despite his poor health and communication difficulties, Stephen still travelled around the world well into his seventies, talking about his books and inspiring people all over the world to think about our planet and the possibilities of the universe.

One last book was also published after his death, *Brief Answers to the Big Questions*, which tackles where our planet is headed and what we can do about it.

OUTSIDE SCIENCE

Politics

Although the universe often occupied his thoughts, Stephen was also very interested in politics. He was a lifelong supporter of the British Labour Party, and although he was English and couldn't vote in the United States, he spoke publicly in America on behalf of the Democrats.

Stephen was very against the concept of war as a solution for problems. In 2003, Stephen called President Bush's order for the US army to attack Iraq a "criminal act". Also, Stephen saw nuclear weapons as a huge threat and campaigned to have them banned.

Stephen's interest in politics meant that he met lots of interesting people. He was invited to Moscow to debate physics with Russian scientists, but once there they also talked and argued about politics! He met Nelson Mandela, the great South

African civil rights leader and president, and was also invited by former US president, Bill Clinton, to be part of a series of talks at the White House, called the "Millennium Evening Series".

STEPHEN SAID...

"MANKIND'S GREATEST ACHIEVEMENTS HAVE COME ABOUT BY TALKING, AND ITS GREATEST FAILURES BY NOT TALKING."

In the UK, Stephen spoke out against Brexit before the British people voted. He said that the future of young people will depend on new developments in science and technology, and he believed that breaking with Europe would damage British scientific research, as free movement of people is necessary for producing and spreading ideas.

WHAT IS BREXIT?

In 2016, the people of Britain voted to give the UK more independence by leaving the European Union (EU). It's a very complicated issue, which even the politicians struggle to understand, but basically it means that all of our economic and social ties with Europe will be broken and Britain will need to build new partnerships with other countries. However, leaving the EU has proved to be very difficult and led to years of argument about whether it is the right thing to do.

Health

Stephen believed that the UK government should do more to help the poor and he was outspoken on issues around disabled people and education. He wanted future generations to benefit from the free National Health Service (NHS) in the UK in the way that he had.

He was aware that without it he probably would not have lived so long, and he was very worried that the NHS was disappearing as parts of it were sold off. He blamed the Conservative government for not investing enough money to keep it running properly and then not being honest about the facts.

But he was also excited by progress in medical research. During his lifetime, great discoveries had been made in the study of stem cells. These are the special cells in our bodies that have a potential to turn into any different type of cell, and so could be used to fix or replace damaged tissue in our bodies.

Stephen's disease, ALS, is one of the conditions that could, in the future, be cured by stem cell technology. Stephen believed that stem cells should be used in research. He once visited a laboratory in Los Angeles where scientists were working on a way to slow the progression of the disease that was killing him.

Saving the Planet

While he was aware of many ways that our planet could be harmed naturally, for example by a collision with a massive asteroid, Stephen was more concerned that climate change caused by humanity is one of the biggest dangers that we face. He was worried that US president, Donald Trump's policy of denying that global warming is a threat would cause damage to the planet that we can never reverse. Stephen said that the Earth could become like Venus, where the temperature is 470°C (878°F) and it rains sulphuric acid!

GRETA THUNBERG

Swedish schoolgirl Greta Thunberg (born 5 January 2003) has become a leading figure in the climate change movement. Greta, who is on the autistic spectrum, began skipping school in August 2018 to protest alone outside the Swedish parliament building. The media, such as newspapers, reported to the world what she was doing, and so others began to join her protest. Within months, climate strikes spread to more than 100 counties, with tens of thousands of school children walking out of school each strike day to try to force governments to act on global warming before it's too late.

Although some people criticize her tactics, Greta is now widely seen as an inspiration. She has spoken to many politicians and governments, including the British parliament and the United Nations Climate Change Conference, where she told the world,

"I DON'T CARE ABOUT BEING POPULAR. I CARE ABOUT CLIMATE JUSTICE AND THE LIVING PLANET."

Despite her fame, Greta still protests outside the Swedish parliament every Friday, refusing to stop until her country reduces its carbon emissions.

AROUND THE WORLD...
AND BEYOND?

Our Beautiful Planet

Stephen spent his life travelling across the universe inside his mind. But he also loved to travel our beautiful planet. This started when his family spent time in various countries when he was a child. And then, after his first degree, Oxford University gave him a small amount of money so that he could go to Iran by train, travelling via Istanbul then Erzerum in eastern Turkey, before reaching Tehran, the capital of Iran. He then visited Isfahan, Shiraz and Persepolis, the capital of the Persian empire.

On his way home from that trip, Stephen was caught up in the Bou'in Zahra earthquake, which registered a massive 7.1 on the Richter scale and killed over 12,000 people. He had been very ill at the time, bouncing along inside a bus, and wasn't aware that it had happened because he didn't speak Farsi! He was certainly lucky to be alive because he later found out that he had been travelling through the epicentre of the earthquake.

Space Travel

During his life Stephen visited many countries. But of course, after thinking about space his entire life, his ultimate ambition was to fly into space and maybe even land on the Moon. He thought that no one would take him because of his disability, but in 2017, Richard Branson invited him to travel on one of his Virgin Galactic spacecrafts, a flight that would normally cost £200,000. He said yes immediately.

MOONWALK

The Moon was the first foreign planet that man tried to reach, with the Soviet Union succeeding in landing a manmade object there in 1959. But the United States' *Apollo 11* was the first manned space rocket with astronaut Neil Armstrong making the first historic moonwalk in 1969. In total, only twelve people have landed on the Moon, although many countries have continued sending unmanned spacecraft to gather data.

Neil Armstrong planted an American flag on the moon, and it's believed to still be there, as good as new after all this time. But planting a flag doesn't mean that America can claim the moon as its own. The Outer Space Treaty prevents any countries from owning the moon.

Sadly, Stephen didn't live long enough to travel on the first Virgin spacecraft; however, he did experience zero gravity. In 2007 he was invited by NASA to the Kennedy Space Center in Florida where he tried out one of their special zero-gravity planes used to train astronauts. They are known as "vomit comets" because zero gravity often makes people sick the first time they experience it. Although the zero-G plane was soaring over the

Atlantic rather than into space, Stephen was able to experience free movement for the first time in forty years. He loved it, and the plane stayed up for two hours, allowing Stephen to experience zero gravity eight times as the plane dived.

ANIMALS IN SPACE

Humans aren't the only living creatures to have travelled into space!

• In 1947, fruit flies were the first to go inter-galactic, in an attempt to study the effects of radiation.

• Then in 1957, a dog named Laika was sent up in the Russian rocket *Sputnik 2*, but there was no plan to get her back. Laika died after a few hours in space.

• In 1959, the United States sent two monkeys, Miss Able and Miss Baker, into space. Luckily for them, they were brought home safely.

• Then in 1963, a French cat named Félicitte was chosen for a space voyage. After 15 minutes in space, she came home safely, too!

But don't worry, scientists no longer send animals into space.

Stephen was convinced that space travel would soon become necessary for our species. He believed that the technology was almost within our grasp, and that if we stay on Earth, humans could be wiped out.

DO YOU WANT TO BE AN ASTRONAUT?

NASA, the National Aeronautics and Space Administration, gets a lot of applications from people who want to be astronauts, and they're always on the lookout for crew members to work transporting cargo to the International Space Station (ISS). They also sometimes recruit for new crew to live on the ISS. Tim Peake spent six months there from in 2015 and became the first British astronaut to perform a spacewalk.

The traditional route to space is to qualify and get experience as a pilot or engineer. This is still a good way, but it's no longer the only way. You could now be considered if you have a degree in engineering, biological science, physical science, computer science or mathematics.

Then you'll need at least three years of experience that you can show is relevant to the job, or at least 1,000 hours flying as a pilot in command of a jet aircraft.

You'll also need to pass the NASA long-duration physical. You'll need good eyesight, but they don't mind if you wear glasses.

On top of this, you'll need skills in leadership, teamwork and communications. It's never too soon to plan for your future career in space!

STEPHEN THE STAR

In the Public Eye

Stephen Hawking was a very unlikely celebrity, but he was known all over the world, partly from his many TV appearances.

He was delighted at his chance to be in *The Simpsons* where he appeared as a cartoon version of himself. In his first appearance, he and Homer discussed his theory that the universe might be shaped like a doughnut. He enjoyed it so much that he was on the show three more times.

Stephen was on adult TV show, *The Big Bang Theory*, too, as well as *Star Trek* and the cartoon *Futurama*, where he was a head in a glass jar!

Stephen even had great fun running down the physicist Brian Cox in his wheelchair on *Monty Python Live (Mostly)* in 2014.

He also took part in various adverts for a wheelchair, a wireless Internet connection,

National Savings and Investments, British Telecom, Specsavers, Egg Banking and GoCompare.

Right up to two weeks before his death, Stephen's famous voice could be heard in people's homes, when he played the voice of the The Guide Mark II on the *Hitchhiker's Guide to the Galaxy* radio series.

As well as his guest appearances, Stephen made his own TV programmes about science. On the TV series *Into the Universe with Stephen Hawking* in 2010, he excited audiences by describing how humans might soon be able to talk to aliens, and time travel. Despite his speech difficulties, Stephen hosted shows successfully. *Genius by Stephen Hawking* challenged contestants and viewers to think in the same way that geniuses from the past had to think in order to answer big questions, such as what, why and where are we?

Stephen has also been the subject of many TV shows and films, with two top Hollywood actors taking his role in major movies. Benedict Cumberbatch starred as Stephen in the

2004 movie *Hawking*. Ten years later, Eddie Redmayne starred as Stephen in a biographical film entitled *The Theory of Everything*.

Award Winner

Stephen won almost every award that a scientist can win. One of the most extraordinary was the Copley Medal, which he received in 2006. It's an ancient award that has also been given to Charles Darwin, Albert Einstein and Benjamin Franklin. Stephen was delighted to be nominated, let alone win.

MEDAL IN SPACE!

An astronaut took Stephen's Copley Medal on a trip to the International Space Station just before it was given to Stephen.

As well as scientific awards, Stephen was given some more unusual honours:

• In 1982, Stephen was given an CBE, the Order of the British Empire (Commander).

• In 2009, US President Barack Obama awarded Stephen the Presidential Medal of Freedom. This medal is the greatest honour that the United States can give a civilian (a non-soldier). For a British citizen it really is a huge compliment.

• In 2016, Stephen received a Lifetime Achievement Award at the Pride of Britain Awards for his contribution not only to science but to British culture as well.

Stephen used to joke about the fact that he never won the Nobel Prize for Physics, but in reality he understood that this made sense. The Nobel Prize is rarely awarded for theories, and Hawking Radiation has not been proven.

Even after his death, Stephen has continued to gather honours. Two Russian astronomers discovered GRB180316A, a new-born black hole in the Ophiuchus constellation on 16 March 2018, just two days after his death – they dedicated their find to Stephen Hawking.

JUST SOME OF STEPHEN'S MEDALS

Eddington Medal (1975)

Pius XI Medal (1975)

Albert Einstein Medal (1979)

Franklin Medal (1981)

Dirac Medal (1987)

Copley Medal (2006)

Presidential Medal of Freedom in (2009)

Special Breakthrough Prize in Fundamental Physics (2013)

Award Giver

Stephen chose the first winners of the Stephen Hawking Medal for Science Communication for their work in bringing science into the lives of the public. On one side of the medal is a portrait of Stephen Hawking and on the other, an image of the Russian astronaut, Leonov, performing his famous spacewalk, plus Brian May's famous guitar, known as Red Special.

How Clever Was Stephen, Really?

So, we know that Stephen Hawking was a very clever man. But how clever exactly? Stephen didn't really like to be thought of as a genius.

He certainly knew and understood a lot of things that most of us will never grasp, but he said that everything he knew isn't too difficult for most people, it just requires people putting in a lot of time to learn and understand it, time they just don't have. He thought the key was to present information in a clear way (without equations!), which is something he enjoyed trying to do throughout his life.

Although his school friends called him Einstein, Stephen's reputation as a genius really started when he discovered Hawking Radiation. But genius is very difficult to define. People are clever in so many different ways. Stephen was embarrassed by this title; he said that it was rubbish and media hype. He accused the people who gave him such titles of trying to make him fulfil the role of a disabled genius (though he did joke that he admitted to the being disabled part).

Some people use IQ tests to try and calculate how clever they are, but Stephen hated this idea. He never took an IQ test, and he called people who boast about their IQ "losers"! While he never admitted to being a genius, he did say that he hoped that his intelligence was near the upper end of the range.

YOU COULD BE A SCIENTIST!

If you're worried you're not clever enough to be a scientist like Stephen Hawking, remember that he didn't learn to read until he was eight, and was never top of his class, even at university!

WHAT IS IQ?

IQ stands for Intelligence Quotient and it's a way of measuring a person's intelligence and mental agility by testing them. In the past, people used to believe that IQ was a good test of intelligence, but nowadays it's not seen as reliable because IQ can change over someone's lifetime and it doesn't take into account so many other ways of being intelligent, such as emotional intelligence and creativity.

However, a society called Mensa exists for people whose IQ is tested as being in the top two per cent of the population. People have estimated that Stephen Hawking had an IQ of over 160, which would be the same as Einstein! Stephen was invited to join Mensa but turned the invite down.

It's fitting that Stephen hosted the science challenge TV show *Genius*. Instead of testing for the most intelligent people, it challenged normal people to think in interesting ways about big questions, which is something we can all do.

THE END OF STEPHEN'S WORLD ... AND THE FUTURE OF OURS

Stephen was born on the 300th anniversary of Galileo's death and he died peacefully on 14 March 2018, the 139th anniversary of Einstein's birth. He was seventy-six years old. He had defied the odds and survived a record-breaking fifty-five years with ALS.

On hearing of his death the Cambridge college where he had worked flew a flag at half-mast as a sign of respect.

Messages poured in from around the globe from important people in the worlds of science, entertainment and politics. A tribute was paid to him in the closing ceremony of the 2018 Paralympic Winter Games in South Korea.

The world had lost an incredible scientist and an inspirational man.

Stephen's ashes are kept at Westminster Abbey in London alongside the graves of Sir Isaac Newton and Charles Darwin. At his sixtieth birthday celebrations Stephen had announced what he wanted on his tombstone:

HERE LIES WHAT WAS MORTAL OF STEPHEN HAWKING 1942-2018.

And in the centre is a swirl that represents a black hole and Stephen's formula for Hawking Radiation.

STEPHEN SAID...

IF THE WORLD WAS GOING TO END TOMORROW HE WOULD WANT TO BE WITH HIS FAMILY, LISTENING TO WAGNER, WHILE SIPPING CHAMPAGNE IN THE SUMMER SUN.

AUCTION

After Stephen's death, some of his belongings were auctioned, raising a lot of money for charity:

Stephen's F3 Black Hole wheelchair – £296,750 SOLD!

A thumbprint-signed copy of *A Brief History of Time* – £68,750 SOLD!

Stephen's bomber jacket – £40,000 SOLD!

Stephen's script for *The Simpsons* – £6,250 SOLD!

So, How Will the World End?

In his last years Stephen liked to talk about the problems that the planet was likely to face, both natural ones and those caused by human actions.

In principle, he said, the laws of physics could allow us to predict the future of the universe, but the calculations would be very difficult. He explained that the chaos factor makes everything too complicated. For example, a butterfly flapping its wings in Australia can cause rain in New York. But this effect isn't repeatable. The next time the butterfly flaps its wings the environment will be different, which will affect the weather in another way.

THE BUTTERFLY EFFECT

Chaos theory is a way of looking at systems that are very sensitive to tiny changes. The butterfly effect is part of chaos theory and shows how a tiny change in a starting point (such as a butterfly flapping its wings) can eventually change a large system, such as weather, on the other side of the world.

Stephen talked a lot about the end of the world. The planet faces so many threats that he found it hard to be positive, especially as mankind causes most of them.

Firstly, Stephen said, the world is becoming overcrowded and we are using up all of its resources at a faster and faster rate. Secondly, we have created the problem of climate change. If we add in disease, famine, lack of water, nuclear weapons and species facing extinction, it all sounds rather hopeless. In fact, Stephen estimated that we may have as little as 100 years left. But he believed that these are all problems we might be able to solve if we try hard enough.

Climate change

Human activity, burning fossil fuels and reducing forested land for agriculture is causing a spike in carbon dioxide, leading to global warming. This means that the Earth and sea are heating up, and sea levels are rising. This is bad news for food production, wildlife and our supplies of fresh water. To save the planet we need to urgently reduce carbon pollution and prepare ourselves for the consequences of global warming.

Overpopulation

Over the last three centuries human population has been growing fast, and now we are facing a situation where we use twenty-five per cent more resources than the Earth can replace. Not only does more people mean that we need to grow more food and produce more products and power, but larger populations will make global warming and pollution worse, hurrying the Earth towards an environmental disaster.

Extinction

No one knows for sure how many different species of plants, animals, fish and insects there are on Earth, but they are under pressure. The WWF estimates that we're losing 0.01 per cent of our species each year, which may not sound like much but they believe it amounts to 10,000 species a year. This really matters because every plant and animal relies on others to survive, so if the number of different species reduces, our health and livelihoods are in danger too.

The Four Bigs...

...that could end the universe (but not for ages yet, so don't worry!).

1. The Big Rip: the universe will continue to expand but at an ever faster rate, and eventually it will overcome gravity and will rip apart.

2. The Big Crunch: this is the opposite of Big Bang theory. The Big Crunch takes the idea that the universe is like the biggest star that ever existed, and so could die in the same way that a star dies. One day all of the gravity could pull the universe in on itself and it could collapse into some sort of mega black hole.

3. The Big Bounce: this is an extension of the Big Crunch theory. It supposes that the Big Bang came about when another universe underwent the Big Crunch, and therefore ours will die in the Big Crunch, too. The pleasing thing about this theory is that it helps explain why the Big Bang happened.

4. The Big Freeze: some people see this as the most likely ending. Our universe has been in a constant state of spreading and cooling down since the Big Bang, so eventually it could cool down so much that there won't be enough energy left to replace stars that burn out or for anything to move at all, and the planets will slow to a stop and be left in space completely cold, still and silent and never changing.

Stephen Hawking's contribution to this conversation was the rather comforting "no-boundary proposal", which stated that (in complete opposition with most of his work) perhaps there never was a Big Bang! Perhaps there was no start and will be no end, but there will be a constant flow of one universe into another through glitches in space-time.

Time and Space Travel

We need our governments to think about our planet's future before it is too late.

Stephen pointed out that in the past humanity believed they had new lands to discover, as Columbus did when he travelled to the New World in 1492. But the Earth is running out of resources and other planets may be our only option.

Space travel might sound exciting, but the universe is a violent place where stars engulf planets, lethal rays from supernovae fire across space and asteroids hurtle around at hundreds of miles a second. That's without even thinking about black holes! On average, there is an asteroid strike every 20 million years, and Stephen warned that we should have an alternative planet in case this happens again. We should not, he said, have all of our eggs in one basket, or on one planet.

LIVING THE LUNAR LIFE?

Many people have dreamt about living on the Moon. But there would be huge problems to overcome first! There's no air on the Moon for a start, so we couldn't breathe naturally. There's only a small amount of gravity, which would be fun at first, but our muscles would soon weaken and our bones would become brittle.

The temperatures on the Moon are what you might call variable, going from a high of 106°C (224°F), right down to minus -183 °C (-298°F) in a single day (you'd be frozen solid). There may be no rain, but we would need some sort of protection from the micro-meteoroids that shower down. And since there's no atmosphere, the Sun's rays would fry our delicate human skin.

That's if we could overcome the issue of "regolith", which is a jagged dust that covers the Moon's loose forty-mile-deep surface, and which damages people and equipment and would make building roads, homes and everything we need to live very difficult.

Although the Moon may never make a

comfortable home for people, or even a nice place for a holiday, it would still be worth building a hub there for research and maybe as a facility for travel further afield.

Is Time Travel Possible?

In books and movies people often travel through time to put wrongs right, change the course of history or just get rich! But, as Stephen pointed out, if time travel is possible, why hasn't someone come back from the future to tell us how to do it?

It *could* happen. Einstein's theory of relativity showed us that the time and position at which we experience an event depends on the speed we are moving. So, if we moved fast enough we could go backwards relative to the time of another person. Unfortunately, we would need a spaceship that

could go faster than the speed of light, which travels at 299,792 kilometres (or 186,282 miles) per second in a perfect vacuum (which is impossible!), and our super spacecraft would take an infinite amount of power.

Stephen said that we should also think about how to travel quickly in space. The only way he could see man doing this was via wormholes. We would need to warp space-time the opposite way to connect two sides of the galaxy and make a shortcut (to get an image of this, bend a piece of paper and poke a pencil through to connect the two sides). You could, he said, even manage to travel back in time with a single wormhole if its two ends were moving relative to each other.

Although Stephen enjoyed thinking about time travel, he did not believe that it would ever happen. But he set up a time travel experiment on his show *Into the Universe with Stephen Hawking*, where he threw a party for time travellers complete with champagne waiting on ice. However, to ensure he only got genuine time travellers Stephen didn't send out invitations until the next day!

He was disappointed that no one showed up, but not surprised because he said that if general relativity is correct, and energy density is positive (time machines are often said to use a strange matter with negative energy density, which hasn't yet been proven to exist), time travel is not possible.

He decided that although we can't rule out time travel, it's probably best that we don't ever figure it out, because it would cause great problems. However, he did say that science fiction fans should not give up hope; string theory might one day produce an answer!

STEPHEN SAID...

Stephen quoted this limerick to explain time travel:

There was a young lady of Wight,
Who travelled much faster than light;
She departed one day,
In a relative way,
And arrived on the previous night.

Aliens and Computers

He may not have believed in time travel, but Stephen talked a lot about aliens. He even helped to launch an initiative in 2015 to search for extra-terrestrial life. He was convinced that intelligent life had to exist in the universe outside of Earth. So why, he asked, have we never seen, met or been invaded by aliens?

Maybe, he wondered, it was that the chances of life suddenly springing up on another planet were too small. Or, if life had appeared, maybe it wasn't intelligent life. Perhaps it was because of asteroids? If, on average, every 20 million years there is a collision, perhaps the life forms on other planets, like the dinosaurs on Earth, did not have a chance to develop before the next big hit.

A third idea Stephen had was that when intelligent life forms it tends to develop to a certain level before it destroys itself. He hoped that this wasn't true, and preferred a fourth option – that there is intelligent life out there but they are just not interested in us!

Could Computers Take Over?

Stephen believed there wasn't much difference between how the brain of an earthworm works and how artificial intelligence (AI) like computers and robots works. Just as an earthworm could evolve into a more intelligent species, one day computers could become as intelligent as humans. In fact, if Moore's law, which states that computers double their capacity every two years, continues to be true, computers will become more intelligent than humans sometime over the next hundred years.

When computers become better at redesigning themselves than we are, we had better hope that they and we are on the same side! Stephen said that ignoring this could be our worst mistake ever and he was involved in several groups that researched the impact of AI on our lives.

SEEING DOUBLE?

Have you ever wished you had a double so you could be in two places at once? Stephen believed that realistic 'digital surrogates' could one day be a reality and you could be at home doing homework at the same time as you're at the movies with your friends!

The benefits of AI for the human race are huge. Just as Stephen relied on computers to generate his voice and give him mobility, we are already seeing potential for intelligent computers that can drive cars and win chess games against master human players. But AI weapons are also in development, which shows that super-intelligence AI could be the worst thing to happen to us. But – as Stephen proved to us all – we must not fear change, we must plan ahead and make it work in our favour.

LAST WORDS

The final chance to hear Stephen's voice will only be available to aliens! His words, a message of peace, hope and unity set to music by composer Vangelis, will be beamed into space towards our nearest black hole, 1A 0620-00. Who knows who may be out there listening?

A NOTE FROM STEPHEN

- Be curious. Stephen believed that a good scientist is always driven by a curiosity about how things work.

- Don't be afraid to think and dream. He advised you to look up at the stars and not down at your feet, and then try to make sense of what you see.

- Stephen's illness taught him to focus on what he could do, not the things he couldn't. It doesn't matter how difficult life is, there's always something you can succeed at.

- When you don't know an answer try to come up with an idea or a hypothesis (a possible answer to a problem which helps you to investigate further), no matter how silly it might seem.

- In science no one ever knows where the next scientific discovery will come from, or who will make it. (It could be you!)

- Not everyone has to be a scientist, but everyone should engage with science and technology and be keen to learn more.

- There are no limits to what life and intelligence can achieve in this beautiful universe.

Look up at the stars (and the planets too!)

You don't need a telescope or binoculars to start getting to know the heavens. If the sky is clear there's a lot you can see with the naked eye.

Stars are most easily spotted, but the brightest objects you might see may not actually be stars. Some planets, such as Venus, can look like stars. That's why, before you head out, it's good to get familiar with the shape of groups of stars, called constellations. Once you find one, it's usually easier to find the others. For example, if you find the Big Dipper, you'll spot Leo, which is next to it,

and next to Leo you can see Virgo.

If you're very lucky, during the summer months you may be able to see the Milky Way, which will appear as a murky white glow. And without binoculars or a telescope you can often see Mars, Jupiter and Saturn, though to see Uranus, Neptune and Pluto you'll need a telescope.

If you time it right you can spot the ISS, where Tim Peake was stationed, zooming past at 27,600 kilometres (or 17,000 miles) an hour. It's easy to recognize as it travels so fast and it's the third brightest object in the sky.

The furthest object that you can see with your eyes is the Andromeda Galaxy (M31). It looks like an elongated, hazy patch of light. When you're looking at it remember that what you're seeing is about 2.4 million light-years away!

Stargazing

Choose a night when the sky is dark, dry and still. If possible go where there is the least pollution. Hills are good as they raise you above the city lights and smog.

You may also want to check the phase of the Moon. A bright, full moon can obscure the stars, but make the experience very dramatic. A late rising or early setting moon is not the best time to stargaze, though you will still see interesting phenomena.

When looking at the night sky it can take some time to "tune in" to what you're seeing so make sure you go prepared in warm clothes. Maybe bring something comfortable to lie down on, as you'll get a tired neck if you're tipping your head upwards for too long.

Don't forget to take a map of the stars that relates to where you live. Or, if you can, download a special stargazing phone or tablet app. Your camera will search for the constellations above you, and tell you what you are seeing.

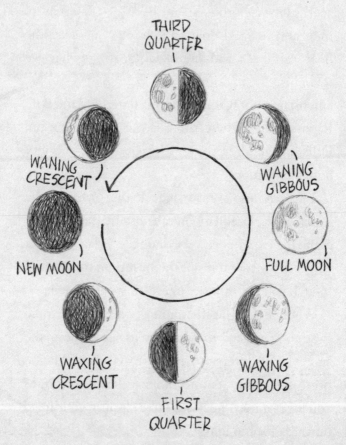

THIRD QUARTER

WANING CRESCENT

WANING GIBBOUS

NEW MOON

FULL MOON

WAXING CRESCENT

WAXING GIBBOUS

FIRST QUARTER

In addition to the Moon, stars and planets there are meteor showers to enjoy. For a really impressive show find out when a full meteor shower is expected. They happen when the Earth passes through the path of a comet and as the comet orbits near the Sun it begins to melt and to shed dust and chunks of rock. The heat vaporises the meteors, creating what we recognise as shooting stars.

Millions of these meteorite particles collide with our atmosphere every day and night, though we can only spot them at night. The best way to experience them is to look at a small part of the sky. If you concentrate you are likely to see a shooting star every ten to fifteen minutes.

WHERE TO STARGAZE ALL OVER THE WORLD!

Møn and **Nyord** (Denmark)

Eifel National Park (Germany)

Bükk National Park (Hungary)

Ballycroy National Park and Wild Nephin Wilderness (Ireland)

Lauwersmeer National Park (Netherlands)

Albanyà (Spain)

Warrumbungle National Park (Australia)

Iriomote-Ishigaki National Park (Japan)

Yeongyang Firefly Eco Park (South Korea)

Cherry Springs State Park (USA)

Death Valley National Park (USA)

Mauna Kea, Hawaii (USA)

Best Stargazing Locations in the UK

There are four international dark sky reserves in the UK (Brecon, Exmoor, Snowdonia and South Downs) and an international dark sky park (Northumberland).

TIMELINES

Cosmic Calendar

It's hard to understand the scale of time from the Big Bang until today, but if we imagine it as a year, this is when each step of its development would have happened.

1 January (13.8 BYA*) The Big Bang

22 January (12.85 BYA) The first galaxies form

16 March (11 BYA) The Milky Way forms

2 September (4.57 BYA) Earth and our solar system forms

6 September (4.4 BYA) The oldest rocks on Earth form

14 September (4.1 BYA) First carbon-based life forms appear

29 October (2.4 BYA) Oxygen appears in Earth's atmosphere

7 December (0.67 BYA) Simple jelly or sponge animals appear

17 December (0.5 BYA) Fish appear

21 December (0.4 BYA) Insects appear

22 December (0.36 BYA) Amphibians appear
24 December (0.25 BYA) 90% of species die out!
25 December (0.23 BYA) Dinosaurs appear
26 December (0.15 BYA) Birds appear
30 December (65 MYA**) The first primates appear
31 December 23:44pm (0.4 MYA) Early humans began to use fire
31 December 23:52pm (0.2 MYA) The first Modern humans appear

*BYA = Billion Years Ago
**MYA = Million Years Ago

TIMELINE OF STEPHEN HAWKING'S LIFE

1942 Stephen Hawking is born on January 8
1952 Attends St Albans School
1959 Receives scholarship to attend University College, Oxford
1962 Begins PhD in cosmology at Cambridge University

1963 Diagnosed with ALS

1965 Marries his first wife, Jane Wilde

1966 Wins Adams Prize

1967 Stephen's son, Robert, is born

1970 Stephen's daughter, Lucy, is born

1970 Shows that black holes can emit radiation

1974 Elected as a fellow of the Royal Society

1975 Wins Eddington and Pius XI medals for science

1979 Becomes Lucasian Professor of Mathematics at Cambridge

1979 Stephen's son, Tim, is born

1982 Awarded CBE

1985 Develops pneumonia and loses his speech

1988 Publishes *A Brief History of Time*

1989 Made a Companion of Honour by Queen Elizabeth II

1993 Publishes *Black Holes and Baby Universes and other Essays*

1993 Stephen Spielberg produces a documentary about him

1995 Marries his nurse, Elaine Mason

1998 Publishes *Stephen Hawking's Universe: The Cosmos Explained*

2001 Publishes *The Universe in a Nutshell*

2002 Publishes *On the Shoulders of Giants*

2004 Announces that he has solved the Black Hole paradox

2007 Divorces Elaine Mason

2007 Enjoys a weightless flight in the United States

2014 Oscar-winning movie *The Theory of Everything* is released

2015 Supports new project to search for alien intelligence

2018 Dies on 14 March

TIMELINE OF SCIENCE AND TECHNOLOGY

1943 Colossus, the first programmable, electronic, digital computer created

1945 Nuclear bombs dropped on Japan

1951 The first video recorder invented

1953 The discovery of the structure of DNA

1962 The first computer game invented

1964 BASIC computer code developed

1967 The first calculators produced

1969 Man lands on the Moon

1969 Concorde's first flight

1971 First spacecraft lands on Mars

1971 LCD screens invented

1977 MRI body scanning invented

1984 3D printers invented

1988 The first cell phones invented

1985 Toshiba produces first laptop

1990 The World Wide Web is launched

1990 Hubble Space Telescope sent into orbit

1997 Dolly the sheep cloned

2001 The iPod launched

2005 YouTube launched

2007 First iPhone announced

2008 Android OS cell phones produced

2010 First iPad released

2012 Higgs boson discovered

2012 Curiosity rover lands on Mars

2014 First autonomous car on sale

2016 A possibly habitable planet in the Alpha Centauri system discovered

BIBLIOGRAPHY AND FURTHER READING

Aderin-Pocock, Maggie and DK (2014)
The Planets: The Definitive Visual Guide to our Solar System,
Dorling Kindersley

Edwards, Chris (2017)
All About Stephen Hawking,
Blue River Press

Ferguson, Kitty (2017)
Stephen Hawking: His Life and Work,
Bantam Press

Hawking, Lucy and Hawking, Stephen (2007)
George's Secret Key to the Universe,
Simon & Schuster

Hawking, Stephen (2013)
My Brief History,
Bantam Press

Hawking, Stephen (2018)
Brief Answers to the Big Questions,
Hodder & Stoughton

Hawking, Stephen, with Mlodinow, Leonard (2005),
The Grand Design,
Bantam Books

Newland, Sonya (2015)
Inspirational Lives: Stephen Hawking,
Wayland

Ó Briain, Dara (2017)
Beyond the Sky: You and the Universe,
Scholastic

Pettman, Kevin (2018)
Space Number Crunch!,
Carlton

GLOSSARY

Amyotrophic Lateral Sclerosis (ALS): a disease that destroys the neurons controlling muscles, leaving the sufferer paralyzed

Astronomy: the study of planets, stars and other objects in space

Atom: the basic building block for all matter in the universe, made up of tiny particles called protons, neutrons and electrons

Big Bang theory: the theory which states that the universe expanded out of a single, tiny point 13.8 billion years ago and has continued growing ever since

Biology: the study of everything living

Black holes: a region in space with gravity so strong that everything, even light, is sucked inside

BYA: billion years ago

Caltech: the California Institute of Technology

Chemistry: the study of matter and what it is made from

Cosmology: the study of the beginning, the evolution and the future of the universe

Coxswain: the member of a rowing team who steers and keeps the rowers in rhythm

Dark matter: an invisible matter that makes up 90 percent of the matter in the universe

Doctorate: the highest level university degree, after which a person can be called a doctor. Also called a PhD

Electron: one of the tiny particles that makes up an atom, electrons have a negative charge.

Energy: a way to measure how an object can do work or make a change. It can't be created or destroyed, but can be changed from one type to another

Epidemiologist: a person who studies disease

Galaxy: a group of billions of planets, stars, gas and dust, held together by gravity

Gravity: a force that tries to pull objects towards each other

Hawking Radiation: particles that escape from a black hole
International Space Station (ISS) A laboratory which has been orbiting Earth since 2000

Laws of physics: facts that scientists have understood and agreed about the physical world

Lecture: a lesson at university

Light year: 5.88 trillion miles / 9.5 trillion kilometres, based on how far light could travel in a year

Mass: the amount of matter in an object

Matter: anything that has mass and takes up space is made up of matter

Milky Way: the name of the galaxy we live in

Moon: a natural object that orbits a planet

MYA: million years ago

Neutron: a tiny particle with no electrical charge, found in the nucleus of nearly all atoms

Nucleus: the centre of an atom which contains particles called protons and neutrons

Orbit: the path that an object such as a planet or a spacecraft takes around a star, planet or moon

Oxbridge: a name given to the two universities at Oxford and Cambridge

Particle: tiny bits of matter that make up everything

PhD: the highest level university degree, after which a person can be called a doctor. Also called a doctorate

Photons: a type of particle and a basic unit of all light

Physics: the part of science that studies matter and energy

Postgraduate: a more advanced university degree that people take after an undergraduate (first) degree

Proton: a tiny particle with a positive electrical charge found in the nucleus of all atoms

Quantum physics: the study of the tiny particles inside atoms

Radiation: energy moving from one place to another in waves or particles

Scholarship: money given to students to help with their education

Singularity: an object with so much gravity it condenses everything inside it down to a single point

Solar system: our solar system is the Sun and the objects that orbit it, including the Earth and the Moon

Space-time: the idea that space and time are not separate

Spaghettification: the stretching and squeezing of an object by gravity into a long, thin shape

Speed of light: 186,282 miles / 299,792 km a second

Star: a ball of gas (mainly hydrogen and helium) held together by its own gravity

Steady-state theory: a general theory that holds that the universe has no beginning or end but remains much the same throughout time.

Stem cells: cells in our bodies which do not yet have a purpose, so could become any type of cell

Subatomic: smaller than an atom

Subatomic particle: a particle smaller than an atom

Sun: our Sun is just one of hundreds of billions of stars in the Milky Way Galaxy

Theory: an explanation of an aspect of the world based on research and provable facts

Universe: all of the galaxies. In short, everything

Wavelength: the measured distance between the peaks of two back-to-back waves

INDEX

WHY NOT READ
KATHERINE JOHNSON BY
LEILA RASHEED...

KATHERINE JOHNSON

There will always be SCIENCE, ENGINEERING and TECHNOLOGY.

And there will always, always be MATHEMATICS

A LiFE STORY

NASA Mathematician

THE WATCHERS

The Eagle Has Landed

You could watch by standing outside at night and staring up at the Moon's blotchy disc in the sky – so familiar and yet suddenly so fascinating. You could watch from the comfort of your living room, if your family had a TV. In Britain, more likely than not, you all crowded into the living room of the one family on your street that was lucky enough to own a television set. Even if you couldn't watch, you could listen to the live broadcast on the radio. One way or another, the whole world was paying attention. The event that was being broadcast, live, was a "first" in human history – perhaps the most astonishing first ever.

More than 384,000 kilometres (238,000 miles) above the heads of every other living being, two men in a metal capsule were travelling at over 609 metres (2,000 ft) per second. They were about to try to do something no one else had ever achieved. They were trying to land on the Moon.

The capsule they were travelling in was called *Eagle*. It had been launched into space over four days before, on a rocket called *Saturn V* that took off from Florida, USA. The two men in *Eagle* – astronauts Buzz Aldrin and Neil Armstrong – had spent more than four days hurtling through lifeless, airless outer space to get to the Moon. They, along with a third astronaut, Michael Collins, who remained behind on the command module, had slept, eaten and gone to the toilet in a tiny, cramped metal box. If they managed to land on the Moon, it would still take them four days to get back. There was plenty of opportunity for the mission to go terribly wrong.

If it did go wrong – as other missions had gone wrong in the past – the 530 million watchers would not be seeing the most astonishing first ever, but a tragedy. If the mission failed, not only would it be a crushing disappointment for the USA, but also for anyone who had ever dreamed of a future beyond Earth. Manned missions to the Moon took money: 25.4 billion dollars (actual cost at the time), to be exact. They also took time. The goal of a lunar landing had been announced ten years earlier – for a decade, the government had poured huge amounts of money and resources into this near-impossible project. If this mission went wrong, spectacularly and on live television, it would be disastrous.

If it went right, it would be the first time that any human being had set foot on ground that wasn't part of planet Earth. If it went right, it meant almost anything was possible. It meant that Earth was not the end for humanity, but the beginning.

The Watchers

Throughout history, humans have looked to the sky for answers. Early civilizations followed the "movements of the stars" – of course, it was actually Earth that was moving! From their observations of the stars' different positions, they found out about time and the seasons. By watching the stars, whose apparent movements were regular and predictable from year to year, they discovered when to plant seeds so their crops didn't fail. Some of their observations only ended in more mystery – they marvelled at an eclipse or comet and wondered what it foretold.

One way or another, for millennia, humans have looked at the night sky to see the future. Now, they were seeing their future in the night sky again, but this time it was different. Mystery after mystery had been explained, understood and led to new discoveries and knowledge. Advances in science and technology had put men – and one woman – into outer space before, but for the first time, with the flight of *Apollo 11*, humans were going to set foot on an alien world ... if it all went right.

The lunar module, steered by Neil Armstrong to a safe landing place, touched down gently on the Moon's surface.

A few moments later Neil Armstrong announced,

"THE EAGLE HAS LANDED."

530 million people breathed a sigh of relief.

The live broadcast continued, in flickering black and white. The sound was crackly and there were long silences as the astronauts prepared for descent. Finally, Neil Armstrong, in a bulky spacesuit, appeared at the door and climbed awkwardly down the ladder, the weak gravity of the Moon making it look a little as if he was climbing into a swimming pool. His foot touched the Moon, and his next words went down in history:

"THAT'S ONE SMALL STEP FOR (A) MAN, ONE GIANT LEAP FOR MANKIND."

Did Neil Armstrong say the word "a", or did he stumble over his lines and turn the first words spoken on the Moon into nonsense? There would be decades of argument and research to follow. But right then, it hardly mattered. In a single moment, Neil Armstrong and his companions had become the public faces of space. The date was 20 July 1969, and there were men on the Moon for the first time ever.

THE FIRST MOON LANDING

- Twenty per cent of the world's population watched the live broadcast of the Moon landing. It was the biggest audience for a live broadcast ever at that time.

- Do you know anyone who watched the event live? Why not ask your parents or grandparents if they saw it?

- You can watch the Moon landing here: **nasa.gov/multimedia/hd/apollo11_hdpage.html**

NOTES

....

....

....

....

....

....

....

....

....

....